ON LITERARY WORLDS

ON LITERARY WORLDS

Eric Hayot

OXFORD
UNIVERSITY PRESS

OXFORD
UNIVERSITY PRESS

Oxford University Press is a department of the University of Oxford.
It furthers the University's objective of excellence in research,
scholarship, and education by publishing worldwide.

Oxford   New York
Auckland   Cape Town   Dar es Salaam   Hong Kong   Karachi
Kuala Lumpur   Madrid   Melbourne   Mexico City   Nairobi
New Delhi   Shanghai   Taipei   Toronto

With offices in
Argentina   Austria   Brazil   Chile   Czech Republic   France   Greece
Guatemala   Hungary   Italy   Japan   Poland   Portugal   Singapore
South Korea   Switzerland   Thailand   Turkey   Ukraine   Vietnam

Oxford is a registered trademark of Oxford University Press
in the UK and certain other countries

Published in the United States of America by
Oxford University Press
198 Madison Avenue, New York, NY 10016

Library of Congress Cataloging-in-Publication Data
Hayot, Eric, 1972–
On literary worlds / Eric Hayot.
p. cm.
ISBN 978–0–19–992669–5 (cloth : acid-free paper)
1. Literature.   I. Title.
PN45.H388 2012
808—dc23
2012002521

ISBN 978–0–19–992669–5

1 3 5 7 9 8 6 4 2
Printed in the United States of America
on acid-free paper

CONTENTS

CONTENTS

ACKNOWLEDGMENTS

I am more grateful than usual to my friends and colleagues for this book. Over the course of the last three years I have exceeded in a variety of social media and locations (dinners, e-mail, hotel rooms, airport lounges, walks, phone calls) the amount of time that you're allowed to talk about your book with other people without becoming obnoxious. That I still have friends is a testament to their patience and generosity; colleagues, probably to the terrible academic job market.

I do not know how other people get their books done, or not really. There's something very private about it. That said I feel like my process is more communitarian than most. In the earliest days, and then later and later again, hours-long conversations with Steven Yao, Chris Bush, Pericles Lewis, Mark Goble, Rebecca Walkowitz, Elisa Tamarkin, and Sianne Ngai crystallized the book's first ideas. A number of other friends read parts or whole chapters. Haun Saussy once again served as a library of references, extensions, creative leaps and clever asides, Timothy Billings as an example of conscientious thinking and careful reading, Sophia McClennen as a figure of necessary suspicion and even more necessary support. Brian Lennon and Nergis Ertürk talked me out of a pages-long rhetorical error. Ronnie Hsia and Sophie de Schaepdrijver and I drank our way around the book one evening; Chris Reed and Chris Castiglia and I, a couple afternoons. Susan Stanford Friedman, fellow traveler, has been a conversation partner about this and other projects. Jon Abel helped me make a Greimasian square. As I was writing, I taught a series of graduate classes (theories of globalization; virtual worlds; concepts of modernity; prose fiction) that allowed me to work through the concerns the book develops. I'm grateful to the students in those classes for their energy, inventiveness, and imagination, which cleared paths through many a thicket.

A number of other folks read parts of the manuscript, or talked through its ideas. They include Françoise Lionnet, Jing Tsu, Yomi Braester, Anne Cheng, Josephine Park, Charlotte Eubanks, Bill Brown, Colleen Lye, Tina Chen, Emily Apter, Mark McGurl, Richard Watts, Erica Brindley, Ted Wesp, Susan Andrade, Mara de Gennaro, Kelly Klingensmith, Sharon Oster, Caroline Levine, Shuang Shen, David Wellbery, Françoise Melzer, Stuart Burrows, Lisi Schoenbach, Venkat Mani, Marshall Brown, Richard Grusin, Ted Martin, Annie McClanahan, Djelal Kadir, Jon Eburne, Tim Bewes (who put me on to Goldmann), Michael Puett, Robert Caserio, Nirvana Tanoukhi, Rita Felski, Bruce Robbins, Jane Gallop, Henry Morello, Dennis Schmidt, Shu-mei Shih, David Damrosch, and Ursula Heise. (That many of those folks are my colleagues helps explain why Penn State is a good place to work.) Near the end two anonymous reviewers for Oxford made some very helpful suggestions. Kevin Platt invited me to give the first major talk on the book's ideas; the members of the audience at the University of Pennsylvania who attended it—especially Jed Esty, Jos Lavery, and Priya Joshi—made invaluable comments in person and through e-mail. Three people read the whole manuscript, more or less in order, and shaped its final structure and tone: Andrea Bachner, Sianne Ngai, and Paul Saint-Amour. I owe them each a special oratorio of thanks and praise. The delightful phrase "don't be a diegetic positivist" is one of Paul's many contributions to the book, and his friendship one of the best things that happened during the period of its writing.

Shannon McLachlan is the one who first had the idea of making a book out of this at all (without her it would have been, apparently, a long article). Brendan O'Neill, at Oxford University Press, has been a mountain of competence, help, and sly humor.

I have been lucky to receive ongoing support and friendship of people in State College, in ways extending well beyond this specific book. They include Tom Beebee, Alex Huang, Liana Chen, Reiko Tachibana, Janet Lyon, Todd Erdley, Michael Bérubé, Djelal Kadir, Michael Elavsky, Michelle Decker (who did the index), Grace Wu (my research assistant), Lee Ahearn, Sean Goudie, Derek Fox, Hester Blum, Ben Schreier, Sarah Koenig, Steri Elavsky, Juanita Djelal, Susan Welch, Sean Goudie, and On-cho Ng. Parts of this book were written during the difficult months following the birth of my son, Jules (who's now doing fine). The outpouring of love and support that came from my friends and colleagues helped, during the bleaker early weeks, make the future imaginable. So, in the middle of apocalypse, did Chunyuan Di.

For her ongoing mentorship and support, for her indulgence of my uninformed questions about the medieval period, for her lifelong dedication to the discipline, institution, and ethos of comparative literature, and for having taken a chance on me the second time around, I dedicate this book to Carey Eckhardt.

State College
Summer 2012

A version of part 1 appears in *MLQ*; most of part 3 in *NLH*. Some sentences from part 1 appear in "World Literature and Globalization Studies" (*The Routledge Companion to World Literature*, ed. David Damrosch, Theo D'Haen, and Djelal Kadir); some sentences and ideas from part 2 are found in "Solomon's Bluff: Virtual Property and the Aesthetics of Modern Worldmaking," which I cowrote with Edward Wesp (*Modernism and Copyright*, ed. Paul Saint-Amour [Oxford UP, 2011]). I'm grateful to everyone for permission to reprint.

ON LITERARY WORLDS

INTRODUCTION

Though literature is not a technology, the historical models literary scholars use to describe literary history owe a great deal to the languages of originality, novelty, progress, and invention that core the idea of technological development. No real surprise: putting progress at the center of historicity is one of the things that makes us moderns. But if you think like a modern person then it's very hard to ever really make a good case for why someone interested in the history of modern literary aesthetics ought to read most of the literature of the non-Western world.[1]

Oh, sure, there are all sorts of other reasons to read non-Western literature. It is, one can say, good for you; it expands the mind, makes one aware of other cultures, teaches the history of colonial and postcolonial struggles. And we would be remiss not to recognize its occasional impacts on the geniuses of the twentieth-century

---

1 In this respect, to be "modern" is to have what J. M. Blaut calls a diffusionist view of history. Diffusionism, "a theory about the way cultural processes tend to move over the surface of the world as a whole," in its Eurocentric variant constitutes the major folklore of Western history in the modern period (Blaut, *The Colonizer's Model of the World: Geographical Diffusionism and Eurocentric History* [Guilford, 1993], 1).

European aesthetic: Picasso was influenced by African masks, T. S. Eliot by the language of the minstrel show, Brecht by Chinese theater, Rimbaud by the French Orient. These things are all interesting, even "important"—you would be hard-pressed to find anyone in the literary academy who thought otherwise.

But that importance has not mattered much to the making of literary history. Despite three decades of work illustrating the explicitly and implicitly non-Western origins of the modernist aesthetic, the masks, the minstrel show, the Chinese theater, and the Orient more generally have never acquired the kind of substantive force or historical importance borne by the more traditionally European prehistories of modernism. Those prehistories extend backward, to be sure, to the Greeks and the Hebrews, where they consolidate the imaginary history of the West as a self-sufficient, self-directed engine of its own becoming. To insist *beyond a certain limit* (namely, the limit of canonization and centrality) on the relevance of the non-West to that picture—to argue, for instance, that without Africa cubism was unthinkable—is treated, in my occasional experience, like so much special pleading. The force of the Orientalist and postcolonial critiques of the imaginary insularity of the West has extended, despite all its promise, only so far.[2]

In my field, modernist studies, the struggle to think the possible relevance of the non-West to the history of aesthetics has revolved around the problem of originality. This owes partly to the explicit

---

2 To some extent this problem, in which an innovative "outsider" critique, widely acknowledged as important, nonetheless fails to deliver the canonical reforms it seemed to presage, follows a model that bedevils all such critiques: though they allow (as do postcolonial theory, feminist and queer theory, or ethnic studies) for all sorts of new work, the very fact of their being named and remarked on *as a field* allows others to put work done under their rubric in a box that isolates them from the centers of literary canonicity. In this respect American literary studies, though obviously too focused on the U.S. mainland until the transnational turn of the last decade, has done a far better job, I think, than have a number of other fields, including modernist studies, in imagining the discoveries of the new forms of scholarship, especially ethnic studies, as central to the field of analysis.

importance of innovation to the modernist authors and their critics, for whom Ezra Pound's "Make It New" continues to serve as slogan and watchword.[3] Though it was easy enough to show how various elements of the non-West (located abroad or in the metropole) affected the intellectual and aesthetic life of European and U.S. literature, none of these elements could substantially disrupt the fundamental faith of the field: modernism was over; it had been discovered and perfected somewhere between 1853 and 1922, and had reached a late second peak in the years just before and after the Second World War. Everything else was just variations on themes. This belief—it is not merely an assumption—has affected not only work done in European modernism's effective past (that is, anything before 1850) but also everything done in its nominal future, so that any artist using modernist techniques (or adopting modernist themes) in the 1980s or 1990s will be considered an interesting derivative of a series of formal innovations already invented in, and perfected by, artists in North America and Europe several decades earlier.[4] The technological and industrial logics of modernization theory, of three-worlds developmentalism, apply also, apparently, in the literary field.

The general theory of progress undergirding that application, in which modern Western art develops new techniques and the rest of the world copies them, has not been unique to the study of modernism. It applies, also, to the history of literary realism, verisimilitude in painting, postmodernism, abstract art, the novel, and so on—indeed across the entire aesthetic history of the modern period from the

---

3 Pound, of course, got the phrase from an ancient Chinese bathtub.

4 The application of the importance of originality was, inevitably, Eurocentric. Sure, Chinese poetry had some neat stuff in it, but Pound's uses of it, since the classics are far away, were acts of genius. Whereas when the *menglong* poets, writing in 1980s China, read Pound and used modernist techniques, they were merely latecomers to the modernist party. See Gregory Lee, *Troubadours, Trumpeters, and Troubled Makers* (Hurst and Co., 1996); and Xiaomei Chen, *Occidentalism: A Theory of Counter-discourse in Post-Mao China* (Oxford UP, 1995).

How is this word used?

sixteenth century forward. It is especially obnoxious in modernist studies because modernism has been so strongly identified with aesthetic innovation, and because modernist studies has in turn made originality the core principle of aesthetic value.

Over the past two decades a series of efforts has been made to expand the boundaries of modernism beyond their usual confines, first by adding women authors (it may seem incredible to students today that Virginia Woolf was once not considered a major figure), then by expanding the reach of modernism beyond the Anglophone. This important task has, unfortunately, usually ended at European shores.[5] Scholars wishing to break open the house of modernism have generally adopted one of these strategies:

- Finding a person who is not widely considered a modernist, and through close reading demonstrating that she or he adopts modernist techniques or responds to modernist questions.

5 For material beyond the Anglophone (but not Europe), see Peter Nicholls, *Modernisms: A Literary Guide* (U of California P, 1995); or Pericles Lewis, *Cambridge Introduction to Modernism* (Cambridge UP, 2007). Bonnie Kime Scott's edited collection *Gender in Modernism: New Geographies, Complex Intersections* (Illinois UP, 2007), a sequel to the absolutely crucial (but completely Eurocentric) *The Gender of Modernism* (Indiana UP, 1990), despite its inclusion of sections on modernism and Africa and colonial and post-colonial modernisms, includes only one selection not originally written in English. A more structural difficulty plagues the recent *Oxford Handbook of Modernisms* (ed. Peter Brooker, Andrzej Gasiorek, Deborah Longworth, and Andrew Thacker [Oxford UP, 2010]), whose inclusion of chapters on various modernisms from outside the usual centers ("Nordic Modernisms," but also "Caribbean Modernisms," "Modernisms in India," and so on) is mitigated by the fact that all these chapters are relegated to a single section—the final one—called "National and Transnational Modernisms." This is how things work: from outside the center, the adjectives and titles are geographically and linguistically specific; from inside, we talk on ideas. But titles like "Architecture, Design, and Modern Living" or "Modernism on the Radio" could probably stand to be rewritten with specific geographic qualifiers ("Architecture, Design, and Modern Living *in Europe*," e.g.), lest the whiteness of the center appear, once again, blank.

- Appending an adjective or prefix to modernism, and arguing that this subtype constitutes a significant new element of the modernist whole.
- Insisting that there are many modernisms, plural, thereby prying the historical boundaries of modernism away from early twentieth-century Europe.

Each of these approaches has the same weakness, which is that it produces literary value by placing authors and artists into an already existing theory of modernism whose center remains European. The only way you recognize that the new person is a modernist, or that Brazilians had modernism, or that the many modernisms all belong to the same general category of the modernist, is if you begin from a conception of what modernism is in the first place. Adding some new person to the general house, which must be done on the grounds that in some sense the person *already belongs* there, allows the same four or five major figures to continue to define its most basic values. The furniture changes; the foundation is unmoved.

The stability of modernism as a category of aesthetic analysis and resemblance may be measured by its canonical curriculum, at least in literature, where a graduate-level "introduction to modernism" course, though different, to be sure, from what it was twenty years ago, still justifies its every inclusion in relation to a theory of modernism-as-formal-innovation established by the earliest scholars of the field (Kenner, Winters, Vendler). Professional requirements for modernist scholarship follow the same pattern, mandating that someone working on Indian modernism or Brazilian modernism or Chinese modernism today know quite a lot about Joyce, Eliot, and Woolf (not to mention Marcel Proust or Thomas Mann), while making no demands that the person who works on Joyce, Eliot, or Woolf know anything about modernism (or anything else) in India, Brazil, or China.

All of this can ultimately be attributed to Eurochronology: to, that is, the forms of historical time privileged by modernity at large, which make it very hard to think past the basic structures that keep European patterns of development at the center of history.[6] Thinking Eurochronologically does not have to be the result of any explicit Eurocentrism. It is not a question of being happy that Europe has been "first" in aesthetic development, as it was first in radio. One may in fact regret such a thing deeply. But as long as the categories governing the profession's sense of literary history insist on the vital importance of such notions as originality, novelty, progress—being first, in short—then we are essentially doomed by the fact that Haroldo de Campos read James Joyce, and not the other way around, to tell a progressive history of aesthetic innovation in which the contributions of the non-West remain supplemental, or constitute thematic appendixes to form.[7] The problem of the non-West's apparent incapacity to generate literary history in the modern period has thus to do not with sexism or racism or Anglocentrism per se, but with the way in which the categories governing the way we think about literary history have made a history of modernism (and indeed of modernity) that included the non-West as an equal partner in its production impossible to write.

Hence this book.

***

On Literary Worlds was conceived in a slightly different order than it appears to you here. The first idea—to create a system of structural

---

6 The term "Eurochronology" is from Arjun Appadurai, *Modernity at Large: Cultural Dimensions of Globalization* (U of Minnesota P, 1996), 30, though I'm not using it in quite the way he does there.

7 This despite, for instance, the fact that any number of Brazilians (Mario de Andrade, say) or Japanese had heard of and were engaging in modernism *well before* many of the canonical modernists did, or that, as is especially true in the Japanese case, the non-Western functioned for the European as a model *of* modernity to be imitated and pursued, and not just as an avuncular and dissipated tradition to be mined for the passionate renewal of the present.

differences around the idea of literary worlds that would allow for a rewriting of the literary history of modernism—appears in part 2. The goal was really to invent a viable solution to the Eurochronology problem, which required a new way of thinking about the historical activity of literature. And because the basic historical presumptions governing the literary history of twentieth-century modernism belonged, as I show there, to the history of modernity that includes it (to, that is, the period roughly defined as 1500 to the present), the solution ended up producing a new way of thinking about the literary history, not just of modernism, but of the entire modern period. If the solution works then what you have here is a way of thinking about modern literature that makes the study of the non-West (and a more generally *comparative* literature) necessary, not on the grounds that it's good for you (at the end of the day, no matter how generously articulated, a condescending argument), but on the grounds that not doing so produces bad theories of literature and bad literary history.

The literary historical model developed in part 2 relies heavily on an argument about shifts in the cosmological theories governing the modern world-view. To support that argument, I needed a better way to talk about literary worlds. The concept of the literary world would then be able to act as a bridge between the large-scale historical claims about cosmological shifts of part 2 and the act of literary criticism as it focuses on a single work, or a collection of works that amounts to some larger oeuvre, period, or genre. A theory of literary worldedness thus became part 1. There, after locating this project in relation to current debates about worlds and world literature, I lay out six "variables" that describe formal aspects of the construction of literary worlds. The variables account for elements of what I call the "physics" of aesthetic worldedness, features of the diegetic sphere that remain largely in the intentionless preconscious of the text and constitute its unspoken, world-oriented ideological normativity.

So, part 1, a language for describing literary worlds; part 2, a world-oriented history of modern literature. They are followed by part 3, which carries the experiments of the first two parts into the literary institution. What theories of history, it asks, underlie the basic forms of literary scholarship, from undergraduate and graduate curricula to academic societies, organizations, and journals, from the job market to practices of teaching and reading? How do those theories shape what we teach and know, what we can see or read? Part 3 shows how the ideology of a normative historicism structures the fabric of the literary profession, and suggests, as I have here, that such a historicism makes certain kinds of scholarship essentially impossible. The existence of such an impossibility is at best a minor tragedy. More tragic is its quiet, continued existence, its silent domination of the ways we think, the ways we read, and the ways we train and teach students.

Together the three parts thus address, successively, the analysis of individual works, their collective arrangement as literary history, and the institutional framework those analyses and those histories shape. They raise, along the way, a number of questions, whose elaboration in the main body of the text would have disrupted the line I was trying to follow. Some of them are, accordingly, addressed in the appendixes, which describe a few stones left unturned. Others need to be discussed beforehand, since they do not emerge from the book, but subtend it. They are thus about the book—about its choices and limitations, about its position in larger conversations—rather than of it.

Q: If this is a book about the importance of the non-West to the history of modern literature, where's all the non-Western literature?

A: Well, here's the thing. In order to build the case for a new way of thinking about literary history and historicism in the modern period, I felt like I had to make the argument work first in relationship to the established classics of the modern European canon—Cervantes, Goethe, Balzac, and so on. Any theory that would allow for a non-progressive model of literary history would have to, as a first test, explain the most central figures in the existing tradition, confirming at certain levels what we already know, even as it cast that knowledge in new lights.[8] The legitimacy of the argument here depends on its ability to address the known facts of literary history, and to alter their position within a larger frame, not in the development of an entirely new frame with its own set of facts. (In this respect the redescription of the premodern–modern transition through literary worldedness, which appears at the end of part 2, matters less to me than the possibilities for analysis that redescription opens up *inside* the modern period, since the former aims to say something we already knew, in a new language, whereas the latter can use that new language to say things we don't already know.) The point is to rearrange the *house* around the *furniture*, to produce the shock of estrangement and novelty within the framework of an internal habitation whose familiarity sustains its relevance and power.

Second, part of the argument is that modernity is a specific historical and social formation that does in fact arise in Europe (and through Europe's relationship with the world); it revolves around a particular kind of world-view that results from that relationship and the encounters that made it. Attempts to describe other modernities, or other early modernities, in

---

8 That the nonprogressive nature of literary influence has been widely discussed (Borges: "every writer *creates* his own precursors") has not significantly altered the general tendency to teach and to institutionalize literature (not to mention history) as though they simply unfolded in progressive time (Jorge Luis Borges, "Kafka and His Precursors," trans. James E. Irby, in Borges, *Everything and Nothing* [New Directions, 2010], 72; see also Eliot's essay on tradition, which Borges cites).

places outside Europe—which are essentially varieties of the attempts to describe other modernisms, and suffer from the same rhetorical weaknesses—do not survive that argument. Accordingly, highly canonical, nonmodern, non-Western works that might have merited some obvious consideration are mentioned but largely skipped over.

As for works belonging to the expanded, globe-spanning modes of literary circulation and production that characterize the twentieth century and beyond (of which plenty appear outside the West), a few of those find mention here, since they belong to the general cultural frame of the modern. Indeed, part of the argument about those works is that they are made newly important and relevant to literary history by the approach I propose. Because the categories I develop are structural and relational rather than progressive, work that under the current literary historicism is considered belated or subsequential now suddenly matters, since the core values of any given literary historical category are not determined by an origin but by the play of relations over time. This also has the effect of suggesting that in the long run the center of such aesthetic categories as modernism, realism, or the novel may prove to be located in our future, not our past—and thus perhaps outside, also, the geographic frames to which they have been restricted so far.[9]

Q: But still: doesn't the whole analysis fall apart if we recognize that "modernity" is itself a limited and obfuscatory historical concept, one intimately tied to the self-regard of the West and designed

9 For a good example of how to do this, see Christopher Hill, "The Travels of Naturalism and the Challenges of a World Literary History," *Literature Compass* 6 (2009): 1198–2010.

to distract us from the historical importance of capitalism? Isn't modernity just a Western invention?

A: Yes and no. Peter Osborne notes that "'modernity' has a reality as a form of cultural self-consciousness, a lived experience of historical time, which cannot be denied, however one-sided it might be as a category of historical understanding."[10] Following Osborne, we may distinguish between the time period described by the term "modern" (roughly 1500 to the present) and the time period in which the idea of modernity became the dominant historical concept of its age (roughly from Hegel, in the early nineteenth century, through the late twentieth century). Even if you come to believe, as some scholars have, that the period described by the word *modern* is essentially a mythology, you still ought to recognize the motive force of the concept of the modern over the last two centuries.

I have largely used "modernity" to describe a world-view that, I argue in part 2, emerges historically at a moment that coincided with significant changes in European knowledge about (and engagement with) the planet Earth and its place in the universe, which date from the late fifteenth century and continue through the Enlightenment and imperialism to the present. For me that modernity exists, not in the sense that it inaugurates a new era of human happiness or historical evolution—it is not, for me, a singular historical origin, or a justification of Eurocentrism—but because we can quite clearly trace significant changes in mentality, in the world-picture, that date from the responses to events of the late fifteenth and early sixteenth centuries. This change comes to call itself

10 Peter Osborne, *The Politics of Time* (Verso, 1995), 7.

"modernity," producing a discourse of itself that, like all historical discourses, constructs its origin retroactively. I have therefore consistently thought of modernity not as an event but as a social concept with its own developmental history, one whose historical spread is highly uneven, not only geographically (inside and beyond Europe) but also socially, politically, economically, culturally, and so on. Whether in this cultural sense modernity is a Western invention or not makes little difference to the analysis in part 2, which focuses on the system of world-relations that the concept generates—imaginary or not.

Q: If you're serious about the literary history of modernity— all modernity—then why is the book so short?

A: The book does two main things. First, it describes aspects of the literary work of art that have heretofore largely been left unnoticed or ignored, registering meaning that the texts have been emitting all along, like ultraviolet light, at a frequency unrecorded by the usual interpreting machines (part 1). Second, it elaborates a series of historical changes in those recorded frequencies, while testing them against a form of historicism whose structural and systematic presumptions produce new ways of doing literary history (part 2).

These goals required that I write a very long book, or a very short one. The choice of the latter foregrounds the necessarily schematic and heuristic system of analysis: I have privileged the conceptual over the descriptive, the experimental over the exhaustive. Writing a short book felt like the best way, for now, to make this set of ideas legible, and to test them in practice. As I suggest in the appendixes, the full implications of the arguments, literary historical and otherwise, extend well beyond work I am capable of doing, or doing alone.

Q: Would it be fair to say, then, that the book tries to provide the source code for an analysis and a task that it cannot complete?

A: Yes.

Q: At times you seem to want the ideas here to apply to the entire historical field of the aesthetic; at times you restrict your arguments to the specifically literary (in the title, for instance). Why?

A: I actually think it's possible that the arguments made here can be extended fully into the entire realm of human making. But I lack the professional training to be able to make that assertion too seriously. Nonetheless it seems likely that the analyses of literary worlds, and the vocabulary developed around both the variables and the modes, could be used to describe the realms of the visual, video, and plastic arts, as occasional brief references aim to suggest. If there are limits to the applicability of the categories here, they seem more likely to lie in the realm of forms practically antagonistic to the very idea of a diegesis—certain kinds of experimental poetry (concrete or sound), or abstract expressionist painting. Here the question would be whether an analysis of world-making at the level of medium or form could compensate for the effective lack of a diegesis, and then whether such an analysis could add anything new to the understanding of the works it described. Just briefly, it would be fairly easy to use terms like amplitude or dynamism (see part 1) to describe the action of a sound poem, or connectedness and metadiegetic structure to discuss (and differentiate) various canvases of Rothko's. Harder, probably, to apply variables like completeness and character-system, which belong more strictly to diegetic space.

Q: Your emphasis on world *as a key concept in the criticism of aesthetic activity feels very much connected to Mikhail Bakhtin's notion of the chronotope. What's the difference between them?*

A: In the concluding remarks to "Forms of Time and Chronotope in the Novel" Bakhtin casually distinguishes *world* from *chronotope*. In so doing he comes closest to describing what I mean by an aesthetic world, a concept that describes the sum total of the activity of the diegetic work of art. Bakhtin writes: the world of a text's readers and writers is "set off by a sharp and categorical boundary from the *represented* world in the text. Therefore we may call this world the world that *creates* the text, for all its aspects [...] participate equally in the creation of the represented world in the text. Out of the actual chronotopes of our world (which serve as the source of representation) emerge the reflected and *created* chronotopes of the world represented in the work."[11] We glimpse in these sentences a theory of world as something larger than a single chronotope. *World* names a chronotope-containing discourse, one that applies equally well to the representational sphere as the actual one.[12] Though Bakhtin does not say so explicitly, we need only take a small step forward from such an analysis to recognize that world is itself—inevitably—a chronotope too; it *includes* chronotopes, and *is* one. This makes it an especially interesting historical and philosophical concept (as I argue at

11 Mikhail Bakhtin, "Forms of Time and Chronotope in the Novel," *The Dialogic Imagination: Four Essays,* trans. Caryl Emerson and Michael Holquist (U of Texas P, 1981), 253. Further references in the text.
12 I have a far less definitive sense of the separation between the represented world and the actual one than the one that appears in these sentences of Bakhtin's. But then, so does he. The next paragraph begins with another assertion of the bright line between this world and that one: "As we have already said, there is a sharp and categorical boundary line between the actual world as source of representation and the world represented in the

greater length in part 1), since it allows us to extend in a number of directions Bakhtin's analysis, both upward (to large-scale issues involving the moving history of world-concepts, or the philosophical being proper to such concepts), downward (inside the diegesis, to sub-chronotopic or para-chronotopic features of representational space), or sideways (to formal and mediatic articulations of worldedness). It is not so much a question of developing *world* against *chronotope*, as of taking advantage of the fact that *world* has in advance of any conceptual description, as we see in Bakhtin's unpremeditated use of the term, a special relationship to problems of totality, of self-enclosure, and of spatiotemporal relations.

Q: Given the scope of the historical field you address here, what happens to close reading? Does doing this kind of literary history mean abandoning actual literature for totalizing or meaningless generality?

A: The balance between the specificity of the instance and the applicability of the general is a problem for all thought. "The delimitation of concepts is different in every language," notes Lévi-Strauss, and "the use of more or less abstract terms is a function not of greater or lesser intellectual capacity, but of differences in the interests—in their intensity and attention to detail—of particular social groups."[13] It should not take too

---

work" (253). Three sentences later, however: "But it is also impermissible to take this categorical boundary line as something absolute and impermeable.... However forcefully the real and the represented world resist fusion, however immutable the presence of that categorical boundary line between them, *they are nevertheless indissolubly tied up with each other* and find themselves in *constant mutual interaction; uninterrupted exchange* goes on between them, similar to the uninterrupted exchange of matter between living organisms and the environment that surrounds them" (253–54, my emphasis).

13 Claude Lévi-Strauss, *The Savage Mind* (U of Chicago, 1966), 2.

much work, however, to recognize that every instance is also a generality, and every generality a potential instance. Whatever a particular disciplinary practice recognizes as a legitimate instance can always be broken down into sub-instances that could themselves be further broken down; likewise any given general statement can be seen from another perspective as an instance subject to a larger generality.[14] "Instance" is not, therefore, a fixed unit; it means something like "the disciplinarily normative unit of evidence considered to be sufficiently small as to escape the critique of over-generalization."[15]

The history of close reading is a strong history of a certain legitimated instance. In that history the instance encodes the specificity of literature: literature is that which escapes the principle of generalization. Instantiation thus generates an ontological premise: it is the nature of literature to be the ungeneralizable instance. Literature's alleged resistance to the social and the normative locates itself precisely at this level of ungeneralizability, through which it models, as Régis Debray notes of the more general epistemological system to which it belongs, "the *eruption* as the superior figure of knowledge, the *pointed* as a norm of style, and the *fragment* as form and stigma of authenticity."[16]

---

14 Even the most general statement of all belongs to the general class of generalizing statements; that class to the class of classes, and so on.

15 What one can say in general, and what one can say about any single instance, are not the same thing. More to the point, there is no guarantee that the cumulative effect of instances will coherently amount to the general. This does not obviate the potential value of generalizations, which intend to express things that are true generally, not to determine the instances in advance. In fact the instance is that which escapes the general by definition. The nomothetic and the idiographic generate different regimes of truth. This incompatibility is a *feature* of their difference.

16 Régis Debray, *Cours de médiologie générale* (Gallimard, 1991), 16, my translation. This principle carries over to wide swaths of poststructuralist theory, including, say, Alain Badiou's theory of the event.

In practice, however, the instantiating nature of literature as close reading imagines it does not restrict criticism's conceptual labor purely to the small or the instantiation as such. The poem, for New Critics; the supplement, for deconstructive ones; or the anecdote, for New Historicists, has consistently served as a mechanism for laddering up from the extremely particular to the extremely broad, from literary instance to highly generalizing philosophical or historical claim. Hence the nearly theological reach by which a New Critical reading of a poem broaches a principle regarding the nature of human reality in lived time (as in the famous discussions of Keats's urn), a deconstructive reading of text or paratext connects its reader to large-scale mysteries of language or being, and a New Historicist reading of an anecdote or private letter manages, from its humble origins, to adumbrate the essential premises of an entire era. What this suggests is that close reading as a form is not, or not simply, a privileging of the instance against the general, but *a particular arrangement of the relationship between the instance and the general.*[17] In that arrangement generality appears as the inductive function of an instance whose solidity and proximity to the living moment of the text guarantees its authenticity, and thus the authenticity of the generality it generates.[18]

To recognize the epistemological and institutional implications of close reading as a practice gives scholars an occasion to

17 The normative arrangement of general and particular explains the immense suspicion among most literary critics toward any models of reading that either (A) rely on deductive or generalist structures, which are felt to "impose" on the literature truths from an idealist outside (Northrop Frye, e.g.), or (B) aggregate large numbers of instances across texts into patterns, and analyze them with methods borrowed from the sciences or social sciences (Franco Moretti, Pascale Casanova, structuralist analyses of myth, or the new "culturomics" work being done on Google's searchable database, for starters).

18 For a longer deconstruction of the relation between the instance and the general focused specifically on the history of "China," see the section called "The Example-Effect" in the introduction to Eric Hayot, *The Hypothetical Mandarin: Sympathy, Modernity, and Chinese Pain* (Oxford UP, 2009), 25–30.

think about the impact of their preferred scale of analysis on the institution of literary criticism. What effects has the dominance of close reading's preferred scale had on the conclusions critics have drawn about literature's languages, genres, or histories? How has that dominance affected canon formation? What kinds of critical lacunae emerge as a result of close reading's demands for slow, attentive criticism of single works, from the amount of contextual information close reading can manage and use, or from the formal complexity required of the texts under analysis? What sort of implications does this carry for the training of graduate and undergraduate students in literature?[19]

Some answers to these questions have been proposed by Franco Moretti, who has coined the phrase "distant reading" to describe the difference made by his quasi-sociological investigations of units of literary production operating at scales both smaller and larger than the individual text.[20] Moretti has argued that the limitations produced by close reading prevent us from ever doing serious literary history—literary history, that is, that would read more than a small fraction of the texts published, or that would understand truths operating at the level of pattern as having the same epistemological legitimacy as those operating at the level of the poetry of the sentence.[21]

19 Among other things we might observe that close reading adopts a stance that takes the work as an end in itself (as though the work were a human being and the reader a Kantian ethical subject), a stance whose model is the poem. Is the novel the same kind of human being as a poem? Are all theories of literature theories of their privileged examples (close reading of the poem, e.g.)?

20 Franco Moretti, "Conjectures on World Literature," *New Left Review* 1 (2000): 54–68. Though the phrase "distant reading" has come into common usage to refer to Moretti's work, he himself has largely stopped using it.

21 This position, though it may seem quietist, nonetheless seems to deal more directly and seriously with the methodological problem posed by the scope of human literary production than a claim that "literary studies requires the largest possible scale, that its appropriate context or unit of analysis is nothing less than the full length and width of our

The book does not take a position for or against that version of Moretti; the heat and light surrounding the theoretical promises surrounding distant reading (or made in its name) are best evaluated by the critical knowledge of the readings they subtend. The discussion in part 1 aims mainly to revise, and move beyond, the odd role that "world" plays in current debates on literary method and literary history; elsewhere in the book, as you will see, Moretti's work on the novel has been exceptionally provocative. Nonetheless, as with every other book, the way I read here constitutes an argument for the viability of my own particular method. Nothing in that method seems inimical to close reading, as the short discussions of a number of texts suggest. But my desire to produce a structural understanding of the history of modern literature may well strike some readers as overly generalist, universalizing, or totalizing. To such readers I reply that the relation between the universal and the particular, the close and the distant, the syncretic and the individual, and the establishment and maintenance of the forms of respect and understanding owed to both, requires continued vigilance, some of which must be done *in practice*. In practice it seems to me that literary scholarship ought to be able to function at multiple analytic scales, and that producing a theory of truth that would describe relations among information produced by various scalar relations to the history of literature, as well as to the literary text, ought to be one of the profession's major collective projects.

human history and habitat" (Wai Chee Dimock, "Planetary Time and Global Transition: 'Context' in Literary Studies," *Common Knowledge* 9.3 [2003], 489). The latter, in practice, is charming enough when it involves the soft Orientalism of Thoreau reading the *Bhagavad Gita* (and the classic turnaround of Gandhi coming to the *Gita* via Thoreau); but it makes it hard to account for the influences that go the other way, as with someone reading the Bible and justifying the torture of suspected witches or terrorists. Is that planetary time too? (See also Bruce Robbins, "Uses of World Literature," *The Routledge Companion to World Literature*, ed. Theo D'haen, David Damrosch, and Djelal Kadir [Routledge, 2012], 383–92.)

In developing a mode of reading that manages the paradoxical relation between the "formalism of the general law and the irrational nature of the individual case," as Lucien Goldmann once put it, I have been guided by the work of a number of critics who, like Goldmann, have struggled to bridge the gap between the diachronic singularity of life in human time, and the equally singular, and equally human, collective modes of existence that those lives together produce. Fredric Jameson's remark that "the function of the universal in analysis is not to reduce [the particulars] to identity but rather to allow each to be perceived in its historical difference" marks the edge of one of many circles.[22] Whether the historical differences and short readings generated here will qualify the method as "close" enough; whether the relativism and structuralism of its methodological ambition provides a useful alternative to progressive literary historicism; whether I have broached the limits of our habitual modes of discourse, or merely reproduced them in different form: these are questions, finally, for the reader to decide.

22 Lucien Goldmann, *Lukács and Heidegger: Towards a New Philosophy*, trans. William Q. Boelhower (Routledge, 1977), 70; Fredric Jameson, *A Singular Modernity: Essay on the Ontology of the Present* (Verso, 2002), 182–83.

PART I

LITERARY WORLDS

Chapter 1

The World and the Work of Art

"World is not a mere collection of things—countable and uncountable, known and unknown—that are present at hand. Neither is world a merely imaginary framework added by our representation to the sum of things that are present. *World worlds*, and is more fully in being than all those tangible and perceptible things in the midst of which we take ourselves to be at home."[1]

So Heidegger, in an essay in which an "intimate strife" between world and earth organizes the being of the world's analogical—or not merely analogical—counterpart, the work of art.[2] The intimacy Heidegger proposes between the work and the world relies, as we shall see, on the flamboyantly deployed quasi-tautology that binds *world* together as subject and predicate of its own tiny sentence. *World worlds.* In the production of this self-same, self-sustaining, self-containing container and sustainer, we glimpse a vision of the fullness of Heideggerian being.

The concept of worldedness Heidegger develops there is taken up and extended by Jean-Luc Nancy in *The Creation of the World*, where "a world is only a world for those who inhabit it," and "an ethos, a *habitus* and an inhabiting: it is what holds to itself and in itself, following to its proper mode."[3] We may as well say, Nancy

---

1 Martin Heidegger, "The Origin of the Work of Art," in *Off the Beaten Track*, ed. and trans. Julian Young and Kenneth Haynes (Cambridge UP, 2002), 23.

2 The phrase "intimate strife" is from Giorgio Agamben, *The Open: Man and Animal*, trans. Kevin Attell (Stanford UP, 2004), 71.

3 Jean-Luc Nancy, *The Creation of the World; or, Globalization*, trans. François Raffoul and David Pettigrew (SUNY P, 2007), 42–43. Further references in the text.

continues, "that the world presupposes itself," that its meaning "does not occur as a reference to something external to the world" (42–43). A world encloses and worlds itself as the container that is identical with its contents and its containing, as a ground for itself that does not exceed or reach outside itself. World is thus (Nancy again) "the common place of a totality of places, of presences and dispositions for possible events" (42–43). It makes, and is, in other words, and in the broadest possible philosophical sense, a physics.

Heidegger's reflections on world appear in the 1936 essay "The Origin of the Work of Art." The energy there generated between the aesthetic and worldedness finally falls, as one might expect from the essay's title, on the side of the artwork, whose being "means: to set up a world," as Heidegger writes. Nancy, in a sentence that you will see again later on, recapitulates and extends the intimacy between work and world that Heidegger makes visible: "it is no accident that art provides the most telling examples" of worldedness, Nancy says, before suggesting that the unity between the work and the art "is constitutive of both."[4]

The relation these two philosophers establish between the world and the work relies largely on the mutual connection to totality governing both objects. The work and the world name a self-enclosing, self-organizing, self-grounding process. This process is neither act nor event, subject nor object; it is the ground of activity, eventfulness, subject- and object-hood, and of procession. There is

4 Heidegger, "The Origin of the Work of Art," 22; Nancy, *The Creation of the World*, 42. What is, finally, the relationship between the world and the work of art? And what, indeed, more broadly, between the world, the work, and the concept of totality that organizes them both? Martin Jay locates the origins of the "aestheticization of totality, in which society is likened to a work of art," in Kant's *Critique of Judgment* (1790–93), where a view of nature (and of history) as embodying the purposiveness without purpose that Kant attributes to the work of art produces a useful heuristic for the development of "longitudinal totalities" (totalities that bring together over time all history into a single concept, as would the theory of history in Hegel) (Jay, *Marxism and Totality: The Adventures of a Concept from Lukács to Habermas* [U of California P, 1984], 47–48).

no common word for what the work and the world share, unless it is "world" itself.

But: "world" means also, for better or for worse, the world, this world, the natural, actual, living world of human history and geologic time. "World" is thus both a philosophical concept and an example of that concept; a concept that is in the deepest possible way an instance of itself. ("Cosmologies," writes Haun Saussy, "have it in common to be self-sufficient."[5]) What we idealize when we speak of "world" as a ground is *the* world's material role as a ground. There is no "world" without the world; the world, as it has been defined, understood, and named (differently) by a wide variety of human societies, is the ground of the concept of world that appears, philosophically, to precede it.

For this reason the philosophical concept of the world cannot alone govern the history of the world of the work of art. While the work is, in the Heideggerian sense, a world, it also *shows* a world, just as the world itself shows a world. Both work and world show both world and its worlding. To focus exclusively on the worlding—as does Heidegger in "The Origin of the Work of Art"—entails passing over the action of the world that is worlded by the work, the world whose practical being-in-the-world acts as both the ground and the expression of a philosophical concept of the world. There is no world-form without world content.

Literary critics have usually, however, focused on the artwork's world-content, not world-form, trusting the general concept of aesthetic or generic form to address the work's relation to worldedness. This pattern of thought means that the world-forming quality of the work, though often sensed or felt, has rarely been directly looked at. Novels, we all know, have certain *kinds* of worlds. But what kinds? To answer that question we may borrow the January eyes of the work itself, casting

5 Haun Saussy, *The Problem of the Chinese Aesthetic* (Stanford UP, 1993), 33.

one glance toward world-content (history, but also the idealized expression of world in the work's preconscious) and another, simultaneously, toward world-form (philosophy, but also the material self-organization of the work as act). Together these two glances embrace the total world-edness of the work, the form of a relation the work establishes between the world inside the work and the world outside it. The history of the world of the work of art is thus always, simultaneously, a history of the idea of the world, and a history of the world as a material substrate, and object of human practice. This book proceeds toward a historicization of the world-concept (and its appearances in works of art) that recognizes that its history is not, or not simply, the history of a philosophical concept, but rather a history of the intersection between such a concept (the idea of the "world," of a physics or metaphysics) and its practical appearance in the realm of human life (the "real" world, the "actual" world, and so on).

Heidegger slouches toward such a historicism in an essay written two years after "The Origin of the Work of Art," his famous statement on "The Age of the World Picture." From its title and its first lines, "The Age of the World Picture" resolutely historicizes the world-concept. Its entire frame of analysis involves the question of an "age," the possibility of determining what Heidegger calls an "essence" or "metaphysics" for a given historical era, one that "holds complete dominion of all the phenomena that distinguish" it.[6] The determining metaphysical essence of the modern age is, Heidegger will conclude, "the conquest of the world as picture" (134).

What is the world picture? Not just a picture of the world. Rather a sense of the world "conceived and grasped as a picture," a sense of the world "set in place before" humankind, imagined "as that for which man is prepared, and which, correspondingly, he therefore

---

6 Martin Heidegger, "The Age of the World Picture," in *The Question Concerning Technology and Other Essays*, trans. William Lovitt (Harper, 1977), 115. Further references in the text.

intends to bring before himself and have before himself" (129). In "The Origin of the Work of Art" Heidegger had written that "world is never an object that stands before us and can be looked at" (23). The world picture is the undoing of that "never," an approach to the world in which humankind makes the world its object, its self-conception, and its history, standing outside it and thereby becoming subject in relation to it.

The appearance of the world picture is, for Heidegger, an event in human history, not an eternal possibility. "The world picture does not change from an earlier medieval one into a modern one, but rather the fact that the world becomes picture at all is what distinguishes the essence of the modern age" (130). The world picture is the modern world picture; it is the name for the modern way of understanding the world, of placing the world "before us" to be "looked at." The world picture is for Heidegger largely the product of the scientific way of looking at things.

That the world picture is historical has implications for the work of art that Heidegger does not address. Does modern art still engage in the world-forming work of the work in general, or does it simply reify versions of the world picture established by the modern world-view? What is the status of the "picture," of pictorialism, in the history of the world-creating aesthetic? Heidegger is silent on these subjects, and indeed on modern art in general. The only work he discusses in "The Origin of the Work of Art" is an anonymous Greek temple. Such an example is well in keeping with his historical analysis, in which modernity breaks the "natural" world-orientedness of the work as such, and, by relegating the work to the realm of the aesthetic, places humanity outside it as its judge and subject. For Heidegger the Fall of modernity is the splitting of the material and ideal aspects of the world.[7]

---

7 At the end of "The Origin of the Work of Art" Heidegger writes that "in its essence, art is an origin: a distinctive way in which truth comes into being, becomes, that is,

Heidegger's work thus recalls how widely modernity is understood as a fracture in the world-idea. This fracture is literal (involving the discovery of the so-called New World and the first European
circumnavigations of the globe) and metaphorical (it [allegedly]
"breaks" the social, cultural, and geographic totalities that had
for centuries governed the European concept of the whole).[8] The
ontological crisis outlined by Heidegger is also a political and economic crisis in the world idea. That is why, in the sentence, "The
fundamental event of the modern age is the conquest of the world
as picture" (134), the metaphor of "conquest" can be read literally
into world history, as a reference to Europe's imperialist takeover
of large swaths of the planet, an event that like the "conquest of the
world *as picture*" seems to both inaugurate modernity, and be it.

Written some seven decades after Heidegger's, Nancy's work
on the history of the world-concept confirms for a new era the
ways a material understanding of the actual world situation can
function as a complement to and subtending force of the world's
apprehension as a philosophical concept. The master term through
which Nancy manages that relationship is, as it is for our time more
generally, *globalization*, a word that indicates the degree to which

historical." He continues: "We are enquiring into the essential nature of art. Why do we
thus inquire? We do so in order to be able to ask properly whether or not, in our historical
existence, art is an origin, whether, and under what conditions, it can and must become
one" (49). The pairing of the notion of an "essence" of art as origin with the possibility of
inquiring as to *whether* art is *in our historical existence* in fact an origin gets at one of the core
paradoxes of Heidegger's ontology. That there might be a gap between the ideal and the
historical is in some sense taken for granted by Heidegger, so long as the possibility of their
coming together exists. That for Heidegger the modern age marks the collapse or the break
between history and ideality, and thus that for him the reconciliation of those two is always
simultaneously returned to a lost past (the classical age) and an imaginary future (whose
prophet is Hölderlin), is a significant feature of Heidegger's philosophy (where it marks a
conceptual weakness) and of his modernity as a philosopher.

8 Victor Segalen captures the sense of circumnavigation as disaster when he writes
that "the first voyage around the world must have been the most disenchanting. Luckily,
Magellan died before his return" (*Essay on Exoticism: An Aesthetics of Diversity*, trans. Yaël
Rachel Schlick [Duke UP, 2002], 64).

the world-concept (or a certain vision of it) has become the open object of historical discourse, a word whose resonances in English, as Nancy notes, seem particularly oriented toward the production of the world as picture.[9] That globalization is itself widely understood to be either the culminating act of a triumphant modernity, or the mark of an epistemological break that establishes a new postmodern age, suggests how firmly the present in both its longer and shorter forms has made of worldedness the voice of its conceptual and material futures. What place there is for the work of art *as* world in the imaginaries of past and present, and what the effects of that place might be on notions of representational space and literary history, are the subjects of the rest of this book.

---

9 The French word *monde*, Nancy writes, "by keeping the horizon of a 'world' as a space of possible meaning for the whole of human relations ... gives a different indication than that [given by 'globe'] of an enclosure in the undifferentiated sphere of totality" (*The Creation of the World*, 28).

Chapter 2

Worlds, Literature, Systems

What is the status of the concept of the world in literary criticism today? One of rhetorically unmatched prestige. This latter emerges not only in the major debates around world literature and world-systems theory, but also, more indirectly but just as forcefully, in the imaginaries and implications of the history of globalization, which touch every dimension of the humanities and social sciences. There the reference to globalization serves as a sign of political, social, and economic engagement (by both the critic and the artwork) that justifies, implicitly, the continued importance of the humanistic study of culture.

It is tempting to reduce one's analysis of this trend, somewhat cynically, to an understanding of *world*'s role as a screen or a marketing technique, an attempt to ensure recognition from the culture at large through the adoption of an impressive scale of potential relevance: nothing less than the entirety of the planet, or, in the case of globalization, than its process of becoming. In the more local context of literary history, the reliance of ongoing debates on close and distant reading (which touch so directly the question of analytic scale) on the word and concept captured by world should lead us to suspect that the debates register far more than a merely methodological shift.[1] However cynically or opportunistically deployed,

---

1 By "scale" here I mean something quite different from what Nirvana Tanoukhi means in "The Scale of World Literature," *New Literary History* 39 (2008): 599–617, where she derives a complex literary critical application for the term via the work of the geographer Neil Smith. For an overview of the history of scale thinking in geography, see Adam Moore, "Rethinking Scale as a Geographical Category: From Analysis to Practice," *Progress in Human Geography* 32.2 (2008): 203–25.

the renewed emphasis on "world" (and *the* world) is an attempt to understand and respond to global processes of economic, cultural, and social transformation. It also points us to something vital, something we have missed, about the history of the literary imagination.

But what? That question will take some time to answer, since it is the fundamental question of this book. Answering it will require, among other things, the development of a type of critical attention appropriate to it as a question about criticism, but also as a question about literature—a form of attention able to address simultaneously the debate and its subject matter, thereby bringing together the question of interpretation (and its scales) with the question of the world, whether one understands the latter as a set of systemic relations, an ethical imperative, or as a habitus and ground for human living.

All that is a long way away. For now, as an opening gesture, observe around the common literary critical contemporary uses of the word *world* a certain critical cacophony, which stems from two opposed uses of the term. In one use, coming from the world-systems perspective adopted (at times) by Pascale Casanova and Franco Moretti, "world" refers not to the actual world but to the total enworldedness, or world-constituting force, of a system. For both Moretti and Casanova, "world literature" becomes possible as the subject of a mode of analysis that grasps it as the effect of patterns of development and change whose logic exceeds that of the individual work, of influence, or of the linguistic opacity of the sentence. (Moretti: "world literature is not an object, it's a problem, and a problem that asks for a new critical method."[2]) The "world" appears, for both scholars, only from a perspective whose distance

---

2 Franco Moretti, "Conjectures on World Literature," *New Left Review* 1 (Jan.–Feb. 2005): 54–68.

from its object permits a sense of its totality as a system of meaning; "world" is not, and cannot be, a feature of the intensive reading of a single work, no matter how representative that work appears to be.

This use produces a concern with explanatory mechanisms that operate at very large scales, that effectively constitute "worlds" of literary history wherever they may be located, and no matter what size they are. Such a concern dovetails with the predilections of world-systems theory. Immanuel Wallerstein has described world-systems as "systems, economies, empires *that are* a world," that constitute, that is, a self-containing structure that amounts to a thing of its own, a definition in line with the philosophical conceptualization one sees in Heidegger. Wallerstein follows his description with a parenthesis—"(but quite possibly, and indeed usually, not encompassing the entire globe)"—that clarifies the difference between the ontological status of worlds in world-systems and their material or ontic ground with respect to the planet (here rendered as "globe").[3] World-systems *are* worlds, in the sense that they constitute a self-organizing, self-enclosed, and self-referential totality; but they are not to be confused with *the* actual world, which—though it is also, of course, *a* world—is the only world whose geographic scope coincides exactly with that of the Earth.[4]

---

3 Immanuel Wallerstein, *World-Systems Analysis: An Introduction* (Duke UP, 2004), 17.

4 Except, of course, that what Wallerstein and others call the "modern world-system," which turns out to be the first world-system that is actually contiguous with the planet as a whole, is the source and origin of the concept of world-systems as such. For competing arguments about the inaugural date of the "modern" world-system (that is, the world-system that is also continuous with the planet), see Janet Abu-Lughod, *Before European Hegemony: The World System A.D. 1250–1350* (Oxford UP, 1991); Andre Gunder Frank, *ReOrient: Global Economy in the Asian Age* (U of California P, 1998); and Kenneth Pomeranz, *The Great Divergence: China, Europe, and the Making of the Modern World Economy* (Princeton UP, 2000). See also David Palumbo-Liu, Bruce Robbins, and Nirvana Tanoukhi, eds., *Immanuel Wallerstein and the Problem of the World: System, Scale, Culture* (Duke UP, 2011).

Another use of "world," belonging to the disciplinary discourse of Comparative Literature, pairs it with the word *literature*, and in so doing aims for a frame for the act of comparison and the problem of human literary history that is as expansive and non-Eurocentric as possible. Over the course of the last decade, "World Literature" has found force in the new anthologies of world literature (first in Norton's "Expanded Edition" in 2003, then in Longman and Bedford, both of which came out with six-volume anthologies in 2004), in several large-scale, collaborative world literary projects (the four-volume *Literary History: Towards a Global Perspective*, funded by the Swedish Research Council, e.g.), and in a renewed emphasis on the term in conferences and journals, partly spearheaded by David Damrosch, former president of the American Comparative Literature Association and now chair of the Department of Comparative Literature at Harvard, who has written, edited, or coedited since 2003 four books with the words *world literature* in their titles.[5]

The "world" of "world literature" is not the same as the "world" of "world-systems." In some cases the terms are explicitly at odds: Casanova opposes her concept of "world literary space," which she describes as "another world, whose divisions and frontiers are relatively independent of political and linguistic borders ... with its own laws, its own history, its specific revolts and revolution," to the "world" of world literature, noting that "world literary space" explicitly does *not* refer to "a body of literature expanded to a world scale, whose documentation and, indeed, existence remains problematic."[6]

5 David Damrosch, *What Is World Literature?* (Princeton, 2003); *How to Read World Literature* (Wiley/Blackwell, 2008); ed., *Teaching World Literature* (MLA, 2009); and Theo D'haen, David Damrosch, and Djelal Kadir, eds., *The Routledge Companion to World Literature* (Routledge, 2011). Damrosch and David Pike were also the general editors for the new Longman anthology of world literature.

6 Pascale Casanova, "Literature as a World," *New Left Review* 31 (Jan.–Feb. 2005): 72. One effect of the Casanovan approach is to replicate the world-systems emphasis on economic and political history as the effect of competitions between nations. As Emily Apter has noted, whatever world literature emerges from such a contest will be the product of an

In the World Republic of Letters, being "worldly" means dominating the world of the literary as defined by and generated through Europe, while the texts and stories of areas not yet dominated by Europe remain, like unexplored spaces on a map, completely blank. Though Moretti has been more interested in the geographic and temporal scope of literary history than Casanova, his models of transnational cultural influence, whether of the Hollywood film or of the realist novel, have regularly adopted a similarly Wallersteinian model of contest between center and periphery, and reflect a Wallersteinian awareness of the ways literary strategies, like novels or nations, compete for survival in markets of literary consumption and pleasure.[7] (The early provocations in "Conjectures on World Literature," where "world" ranged well beyond the limited and systemic, have given way in Moretti's recent essays to more specific investigations on the travels of the novel or on literary methods. In his newest work the term "world literature" has more or less dropped out of the picture.[8])

agon of domination, with each national literature rivaling "the other to become the universal form of a homogenized, capitalized global lit" ("Literary World-Systems," in Damrosch, ed., *Teaching World Literature*, 53). Casanova distinguishes her orientation toward "world structure" from a Wallersteinian world-systems model largely by virtue of her emphasis on domination—but the political valence of the critique does not disturb the scale of its emergence and analysis. See "Literature as a World," 80–81.

7 Such descriptions can become functionalist or prescriptive; if literary prestige only flows out of the barrels of the metropole, then the only reason to read the rest of the world's novels is to see how far they have to go to catch up. Such a position is neither Moretti's nor Casanova's, though as Christopher Prendergast has noted, Casanova's "theoretical frame of reference creates the impression of an inescapably Euro-centric purview" (Prendergast, "The World Republic of Letters," in Prendergast, ed., *Debating World Literature* [Verso, 2004], 9n3. See Casanova's response to that essay in Casanova, "Literature as a World" note 6.)

8 This change reflects not so much a qualitative shift in Moretti's own work as the term's newly charged status in contemporary debate, which makes it essentially unusable for him in this context. He still refers regularly to the "modern world" and the "capitalist world," both uses that remain very much in line with world-systems theory ("The Novel: History and Theory," *New Left Review* 52 [2008]: 111–24). He remains interested in non-European literary forms, and in a global vision of the novel in particular (see *The Novel*, 2 vols. [Princeton UP, 2007]).

To risk "world" in its most expansive form requires, as Casanova and Moretti both know, risking also the meaning of the term "literature." There is no guarantee that this latter term is not the universalizing vision of a European concept inappropriate to the analysis of texts and stories operating under radically different conceptions of the meaning of writing or storytelling—as in the Chinese context, where the word *wen* 文 includes forms of textual production and culture that do not belong to "literature" in its modern European uses. That is why Damrosch and others are willing to risk making both "literature" and "world" more expansive categories, and to insist that any literary history worth its salt will have to take account of a far broader list of works and movements than has so far been necessary under the largely unconsciously Europe-centered regimes of literary study. Though it is always possible that our theories of what "literature" is will borrow from the naturalized frames of reference with which we grew up, it might also be possible to redefine "literature" by including all of its possible avatars, generating a large-scale master term that would then be understood to have any number of specific articulations, some of them, even, belonging to the literature of the modern world-system (a system in which, future historians will report, literature went by the name of "literature"!). The broadest possible conception of world literature modifies the latter term by the former, insisting that whatever we call "literature" would have to be the restructured conceptualization that resulted from a responsibility to the *whole* world, spatially and historically.[9]

In a measure of the very instability of the word *world* in this context, and of the degree to which the term's use in world-systems approaches has muddled its reference, Damrosch in a recent issue of *New Literary History* has been driven to propose what he calls

---

9 For one attempt to do just that, see Earl Miner, *Comparative Poetics: An Intercultural Essay on Theories of Literature* (Princeton UP, 1990).

a *"global* world literature," which would target both the "narrowly bounded nationalism" and the "boundless, breathless globalism" that characterize contemporary thinking about literary history.[10] I'm surely not the only one to find it strange that already by 2008 the *world* in world literature needed supplementing with the word *global,* or to take that felt necessity as a symptom of the insolidity and even ghostliness of the world in its contemporary usage, where it seems to appear only to announce its transformation into something other than what it means, its incapacity to assure the very spatial range it seems to promise.[11]

Between world-systems and world literature, then, a difficulty keeping the "world" in the picture. And not because of a lack of interest or goodwill. It's as though the concept itself were the problem, as though the only way to demonstrate an interest in the world were to somehow leave it behind while keeping it in place. So that a commitment to the world consists of using the term despite the inevitable confusions its use produces, the necessity of noting that one is not talking about the whole world, "all" literature, or even a "place" of literature at all. "Whatever the study of 'world literature' can be taken to mean it can't mean *all* the literatures of the world," Christopher Prendergast writes at one point, which just goes to show that whatever the world in world literature means, among the things it can mean is "not the whole world."[12] Which is, if nothing else, weird.

10 David Damrosch, "Toward a History of World Literature," *New Literary History* 39 (2008): 490.

11 To be clear: I'm not criticizing Damrosch for this. His argument is that the study of world literature itself ought to be global, because world literature looks different from different parts of the globe. What this statement loses at the first level (the possibility of a single world literature) it recuperates at the second, where *global* assures a perspective from which the multiplicity of perspectives (on world literature itself) could be thought and recapitulated.

12 Prendergast, "The World Republic of Letters," 9n3.

So why use the word at all? First because "world," along with its paranym "global," functions in contemporary life as a totem of responsibility to the historical present, itself understood largely as a process of world-transforming whose historical dimensions, political, economic, and environmental value, and actual occurrence remain very much under debate across the humanities and social sciences, and which goes, in most cases, under the name of "globalization." The prestige of "world" as a concept for grasping the presentness of the present is extended and expanded in any number of places in contemporary criticism: when differences between the French term *mondialisation* and the English *globalization* structure philosophical and political critiques of economic imperialism, as they do in Nancy's work; when books on cosmopolitanism as a political philosophy or a literary style stud the academic best-seller lists; when literature can be rethought as an expression of a "planetary time" explicitly opposed to globalization; when "worlding," that is, "building up a life-world palpably disclosing its lived-in modalities, boundaries, tactics, and historical processes," is proposed as a living alternative to the "domineering process of neo-liberal globalization"; when virtual worlds offering boutique, customizable world-experiences present themselves (and are theorized) as specific alternatives to either the dangers or the uniformity of the actual world's single-worldedness; or when a brief furor emerges around a proposal for future collectivities to "figure themselves ... as planetary rather than continental, global, or worldly."[13] Each of

13 On worlding, see Rob Wilson, "Worlding as Future Tactic," in *The Worlding Project: Doing Cultural Studies in the Era of Globalization*, ed. Rob Wilson and Christopher Leigh Connery (New Pacific Press, 2007), 216. On the "planetary," see Gayatri Chakravorty Spivak, *Death of a Discipline* (Columbia UP, 2003), 72; for a response see Djelal Kadir, "Comparative Literature in an Age of Terrorism," in *Comparative Literature in the Age of Globalization*, ed. Haun Saussy (Johns Hopkins UP, 2006); and Spivak's response to Kadir in "The Slightness of My Endeavor," *Comparative Literature* 87.3 (Summer 2005): 256–72. On "planetary time," see Wai Chee Dimock, "Planetary Time and Global Translation: 'Context' in Literary Studies," *Common Knowledge* 9.3 (2003):

these stands among the inheritors of Goethe's first use of the term *Weltliteratur* in 1827. That use, to be sure, was also a response, to the far larger cultural strain of world-orientedness that produced Hegel's lectures on the philosophy of world history (*Weltgeschichte*) in Berlin in 1822 (and 1828 and 1830), Kant's theory of cosmopolitanism, and indeed so much of the thought of the Enlightenment. These authors, along with all their contemporary descendants, point to the importance of the term "world" and its variants to conceptualizations of modernity. The recent rise of world-systems theory in such a historical scenario may simply be a coincidence. But it seems more likely that future scholars will read the conjunction between the era of "globalization" and the rise of world-systems theory as the expression of a more general world-oriented discourse whose social form is one prominent reification of the present.[14]

Beyond this semaphoric importance, which makes *world* such a charged and prestigious term for articulating the history of the present, the word also benefits from a byzantine etymological history of its own. Its definitions in the *Oxford English Dictionary* run to some forty printed pages, and its complexity and slipperiness appear from the very first one: "human existence; a period of this," words whose reference mostly to *time* will surprise anyone accustomed to thinking of "world" as having largely spatial implications. The second major definition makes things both better and worse:

488–507. On cosmopolitanism, see Kwame Anthony Appiah, *Cosmopolitanism: Ethics in a World of Strangers* (Norton, 2006); Pheng Cheah and Bruce Robbins, eds., *Cosmopolitics: Thinking and Feeling Beyond the Nation* (U of Minnesota P, 1998); and Rebecca Walkowitz, *Cosmopolitan Style: Modernism Beyond the Nation* (Columbia UP, 2007). On *mondialisation*, see Jean-Luc Nancy, referred to in the previous section. On virtual worlds, for a prominent (and deeply misguided) analysis, see Edward Castronova, *Synthetic Worlds: The Business and Culture of Online Games* (U of Chicago P, 2005).

14 The importance of Moretti and Casanova to contemporary understandings of the history of the idea of "world literature" can be measured by the fact that they are the only two living critics to whom single essays are devoted in the *Routledge Companion to World Literature*, where they take their places alongside such legends as Goethe, Brandes, Auerbach, and Said.

"the earth or a region of it; the universe or a part of it." Here we are on familiar spatial ground. But what to make of that double "or"? Like the semicolon in the first definition, it forces "world" to pivot between an ontological reference to any self-enclosing whole (what are, after all, periods, regions, or parts of wholes but wholes themselves?) and a material reference to the largest possible versions of such wholes (history; the planet Earth; the universe). By highlighting the tension between world as a generic totality and world as the most total totality of all—the totality of the "part" and the totality of the "whole"—this ambivalence recapitulates the difficulties generated by the "world" of world-systems and the "world" of world literature. From one of its many beginnings (the beginning that is a dictionary, which is also an ending) "world" thus bears within itself the conceptual difficulty that makes its use in contemporary literary criticism so fecund, and so incoherent.[15]

Given this context, non-tautological, precise statements about the world are harder to make than one might think. Hence Ruth Ronen, one of the many scholars writing at the intersection of philosophical "possible worlds" theory and the study of narrative, opens *Possible Worlds in Literary Theory* by defining her key object: a fictional world, she writes, is "constructed as a world having its own distinct ontological position, and as a world presenting a self-sufficient system of structures and relations."[16] The first (and second!) thing one says about fictional worlds: that they are constructed *as worlds*, which leaves us fairly close to where we began.

But the claim is revelatory in its way. Because what the readings of the contemporary use of "world" have shown is that the term is *itself*

---

15 *OED*, world n., I and II.

16 Ruth Ronen, *Possible Worlds in Literary Theory* (Cambridge UP, 1994), 8. Later on, in the conclusion to chapter 4, Ronen repeats this structure: "the reader understands the world textually constructed *as a world*.... The reader also understands the fictional world *as a world* constructing its own set of referents" (143, my emphasis).

"constructed as a world having its own distinct ontological position" (a system, a method, an amenability to intensive or extensive readings) and "as a world presenting a self-sufficient system of structures and relations" (a market; a field of pleasure; an economy of the aesthetic). In these examples, "world" worlds, as Heidegger says, but what it worlds is not exactly the world. Instead it highlights or announces the gesture of worlding, the world-desire. In doing so it eliminates from the sphere of meaning the whole, actual, "natural" world, a paradox that grants to whatever necessarily incomplete world is formed by this naming (or named by this forming) the prestige and power of its metaphorical capture of totality. To world is to enclose, but also to exclude. What falls in the ambit of those enclosures and exclusions will determine the political meaning of any given act of world-making, as it does so clearly in our debates on world literature.

***

World literature that emerges from intensive lecture of a certain type, and remains—despite its global ambitions—compatible with close reading. Or world literature as a literature of world-systems, a product of modes of circulation, requiring entirely new patterns and methods of analysis. In either case the world drops out of the equation. Or rather, it remains in the equation as a *marker of scale*, a figure for the relationship between the method of discovery and the breadth of its applicability. And also, of course, as an asserted connection to the world-oriented historical present. If I had to guess, I would say that the problem is that no one has a very good theory of the world, and that in the absence of good theories "world" comes to mean whatever one does have a good theory of (a system, a method, a social or cultural whole).

Faced with this problem, a task: to come up with a better theory of the world, and of the relationship between the world and literature. Not to produce a mediating relay between world literature and world-systems, but to see if a third analysis, focusing on the ontology of composed works, can bring "world" differently into the scene. And to see, then, if such a theory makes any difference to our understanding of world literature or the history of worldedness as an aesthetic and cultural phenomenon—as a symptom and as a compass for the history, in other words, of totality as a function of the human imagination.

Chapter 3

Literary Worlds

Start simply: *there already exists* a fairly common use of the term "world" in literary studies that speaks to the relation between literature and worlds, and has nothing to do with world-systems or world literature. We speak of "Balzac's world," or "Hawthorne's world," or "Rushdie's world" in ways that rely on two fairly conventional understandings of the word, neither of which is captured by the current world literature debates.[1]

In one use the word names the general social and historical space within which an author lived and worked: Hawthorne in the Salem Custom House of the 1840s, Rushdie in the contemporary cosmopolitan literary economy, and so on. This authorial "world" refers unproblematically to a set of historical conditions whose outlines determine possibilities of literary interpretation, what the *OED* describes as "the sphere within which one's interests are bound up or one's activities find scope; (one's) sphere of action or thought; the 'realm' within which one moves or lives," all of which comes down, once again, to a "part" of the universe and a "period" of human time: a frame for literary criticism that is not itself, technically, an act of literary criticism.[2]

In its other use, however, the phrase means something like the unity of form, diegesis, and feeling composed by the rough totality

---

1 Here we may want to recognize, with Pheng Cheah, literature's "peculiar ontological status" as "an exemplary modality of the undecidability that opens a world," as, that is, a figure for world-imagining and world-creation, which may explain this particular use. I would extend the claim, however, following Nancy, to the entire realm of the aesthetic (Pheng Cheah, "What Is a World? On World Literature as World-Making Activity," *Daedalus* [Summer 2008]: 35).

2 *OED*, world n. II. 10.

of a work: the world of the work of art. The world of a Balzac novel, for instance, is located in a time (the early nineteenth century) and a place (mostly Paris); includes certain kinds of people (the bourgeoisie; the aristocracy, their servants) and largely excludes others (the noncriminal working class); is organized around certain types of plots and social units (the family, particularly the extended family); and so on. You could easily compare, on these grounds, Balzac's world with, say, Raymond Chandler's, and not simply by making the banal observation that one of them wrote novels set in Paris and the other novels set in California. You could start by noting that in Balzac's world the novels and novellas operate, in general, as part of one continuous fabric, in which characters in one novel can appear in another; whereas in Chandler the accumulation of character types, settings, plot lines, and even modes of speech across a number of otherwise diegetically self-contained novels constitutes their emotional and literary force quite differently.[3] This is true despite the reappearances of the detective Marlowe: one feels, reading a series of Chandler novels, that the total stylistic effect of the *noir* world, with its particular modes of speech, characters, and events, operates primarily as an *approach* to the actual world, a heightened awareness of certain of its features, none of which requires the transformation of its protagonist, or a sense of the passage of historical (as opposed to personal) time. This awareness is embodied in the narratorial position and proairetic importance of a single character who lives permanently in, and has been entirely shaped as a personality by, his awareness of the world as *noir*.[4]

3 "The murder novel has ... a depressing way of minding its own business, solving its own problems, and answering its own questions," Chandler once wrote. This restricted, self-interested and self-directed frame helps organize the world of *noir*. ("The Simple Art of Murder," in *Chandler: Later Novels and Other Writings* [Library of America, 1995], 977).

4 This is what I take to be, also, the understanding of *noir* in K. W. Jeter's science fiction novel of that name, in which the main character uses a system of visual and auditory implants that translate all the phenomenological stuff of his actual world into the

By "aesthetic world" let us mean, therefore, the *diegetic totality* constituted by the sum of all aspects of a single work or work-part, constellated into a structure or system that amounts to a whole. Such a diegetic unity need not be diegetic in a purely conventional sense—it need not, that is, be a function solely or partially of narrative development or progress. It is enough that this unity emerges from the interior representational content of the work, and that it thus belongs *as a formal concept* most properly to the arrangement of the work's content, of which it is the formal expression. From this perspective, a haiku has or constitutes a world, even if nothing happens in it—its world is simply the total unity created by the arrangement of its references (or refusals, in some cases, to refer), and by the generic necessities of its season words, turning points, and syllabic length. Likewise the world of classical drama is defined by extension in space and time, and by a relationship between medium (the bodies, the stage) and representation, that constitute its rationalizing totality; while the world of the lyric poem, bounded by an "I" and a "you," spins out its world-structures in the proximities and distances that the gap between them frames.[5]

Aesthetic worlds, no matter how they form themselves, are among other things always a relation to and theory of the lived world,

vocabulary of *noir* cinema, a downed spaceship appearing to him as a propeller plane, a certain kind of woman as a dame, and so on. (Jeter, *Noir* [Spectra, 1999]). Note that Chandler's last novel, *Poodle Springs* (Putnam, 1989), left incomplete at his death and finished by Robert Parker four decades later, allows Marlowe to reunite with Lisa Loring, who first appears in *The Long Goodbye* (1953)—a shift that might alter the structure I describe here but which, given what happens in Poodle Springs, does not.

5 Though narrative in all its forms is far more easily construed as having a diegetic unity than many other types of art, one can easily extend this world-concept as far as painting or sculpture: a painting's world emerges in the spatial unity of visual apprehension just as surely as the literary world emerges in the progressive unfolding of temporal experience. The difference between these forms of emergence may well separate the major types of aesthetic activity, as Lessing argued that it did, but we can nonetheless derive from a painting or a series of paintings a sense of worldedness as more than simply the collection of content, as when one compares the world of Cézanne's still lifes to the world of still lifes by Meléndez.

whether as a largely preconscious normative construct, a rearticulation, or even an active refusal of the world-norms of their age. In this sense they are also always social and conceptual constructs, as well as formal and affective ones. An evaluation of their social and conceptual weight begins by measuring a work's degree of orientedness toward *the* world, the degree, that is, to which it responds or corresponds to the basic philosophical or social world-imperatives of its age, the normative sense of a "real" or "actual" world that bears some noncontinuous (and possibly oppositional) relation to the aesthetic. This is the force, in my definition above, of "diegetic": since the term refers directly to the kinds of content located *inside* the aesthetic world of the object as such, it from the very beginning articulates a relationship with its opposed term, the *extradiegetic*: the world "outside" the aesthetic object, otherwise known as *the* world, frames and worlds it in turn, and constitutes the frame of judgment against which the diegetic content's worldedness will be evaluated. Aesthetic worldedness is the form of the relation a work establishes between the world inside and the world outside the work. The history of aesthetic worldedness is thus always, simultaneously, a history of the idea of the world as such. (Lukács on the modern novel: "What is given form here is not the totality of life but the artist's relationship with that totality, his approving or condemnatory attitude towards it."[6])

The reappearance of the tension between world as whole world and world as self-contained unity in this discussion suggests that that tension might be thought of as a feature of literary worldedness. For while Balzac's world more or less coincides with the lived world of its time (or rather, insists that it does), Chandler's feels

6 Georg Lukács, *The Theory of the Novel: A Historico-Philosophical Essay on the Forms of Great Epic Literature*, trans. Anna Bostock (MIT Press, 1971), 55. I saw these lines first in Timothy Bewes, "Reading with the Grain: A New World in Literary Criticism," *differences* 21.5 (2007): 1–33. I part ways with Lukács later on, when I argue that his statement is true for far more than the modern novel, so long as one recognizes that the nature and concept of aesthetic "attitude" is not a product of modernity's blessed break.

like a restricted or closed-off perspective or framework occupying part of a larger world that may well not know *noir* exists. Though Chandler's world illustrates something of that other, larger world, it remains apart from it. This sense of distance from the world goes a long way to making Chandler feel revelatory. The self-enclosing unity of Chandler's world is oriented partly by virtue of its relationship of difference or noncoincidence to *the* world, whereas the self-enclosing unity of Balzac's work presumes a coincidence between its worldedness and what it perceives as the worldedness of the world in general, so that Balzac's narrator frequently says *life is just this way; life is just so*, the gnomic utterance exuding what one might think of as, without irony, a certain worldliness.

None of this amounts to simply saying that Balzac is a realist, and Chandler is not—though along the way we may well pass through those observations. An attention to the world-creating and world-relating dimensions of their work shows us what *kinds of realism there are*, opening up inside the field of realism (not to mention naturalism, modernism, romanticism, and so on) as a world-oriented aesthetic an analytic category that allows us to describe new kinds of difference and similarity. We might therefore observe the difference between Balzac and what one might think of as a purely neutral or ideological realism, one that affirms without any commentary or emphasis the world-picture it inherits from its social sphere. Balzac by contrast tries very hard to be worldly, as evidenced by both the sheer ambition of the Human Comedy and the endless asides in the fiction itself. Is it realism to constantly affirm how realistic one is? If so, then it is a kind of realism (whose first historical instance is, perhaps, Genji's commentary on romance) that differs substantially from the realism of genre fiction, or from that of Chandler, in whose work the act of self-affirmation (diegetic or otherwise) is impossible. Chandler's realism imagines a double world: a world of *noir* (a "part") contained inside and only rarely intersecting with the "normal" world (the "whole"), whose ignorance of *noir* life makes it contemptible and incomplete. This hard line that Chandler draws between the *noir* world and the one that surrounds it reappears in the formal structure of his fiction, in which the novels themselves are, despite Marlowe's presence, narratively separated and noncontiguous. Under no circumstances are we to imagine what happens "between" the Marlowe novels—nothing happens between them but more of the same. If this is realism, it is realism tinged with romance: dark as it is, the *noir* world is a created one, and the charm and pleasure of the novels is at least partly, as a result, anthropological.

At the extremes a work of pure romance defines its world as a microcosm—a ship, a city, an apartment building—or presents a completely formed alternative to the lived world in which it is produced. So with fantasy, utopia, science fiction. Such created worlds often leave open an aperture to a realistic version of their contemporary world—even "a long time ago, in a galaxy far, far away" stays exposed to the possibility of a historical and spatial reunification of the world of *Star Wars* with the world of our Earth. These otherworldly fictions thus seem to need the aperture or bridge that simultaneously unifies and separates them from the world we know, like the geological gap between the enclosing crescents of Thomas More's *Utopia*—a final hedging of the romantic bet, threatening and preventing the fantasy world's return to, or overlap with, the actual one. In *Utopia* the aperture is diegetic: it was the land's first conqueror who "had a channel cut through the fifteen-mile isthmus connecting Utopia with the mainland, so that the sea could flow all around it."[7]

---

7 Thomas More, *Utopia*, trans. Paul Turner (Penguin, 2003), 50. I am grateful to Michelle Decker for pointing the way here.

Chapter 4

First Propositions

Part 2 of this book will rethink the history of modern literature from the general perspective of the analytic category of the aesthetic world developed here. First, however, we need to acquire a more specific sense of how that category functions, to see if we can account for how, or where, it becomes available to interpretation, and identify some variables that participate in its more general production. For though it is the case that most literary scholars today can speak about aesthetic worlds in impressionistic ways—as I did in chapter 3 about Balzac and Chandler—we have very few specific and common vocabularies for doing so. This is largely due to the abandonment over the last three decades of the varied models of syncretic thought that governed the work of such scholars as Erich Auerbach, Mikhail Bakhtin, Northrop Frye, or Georg Lukács, as well as of those others working in the Marxist-structuralist tradition (Lucien Goldmann, e.g.), or in a less theoretical but equally ambitious Anglo-American one (Joseph Frank, Ian Watt, Wayne Booth).[1] The long, fallow period

---

1 In the 1991 preface to the volume that brought together Joseph Frank's famous essay on spatial form and some of his subsequent work, he wrote, "My preoccupation was never abstract or theoretical; I only wished to say something enlightening about a particular work. I did not set out to write a theory of modern literature, and the notion that I might be engaged in doing so, given my sense of my general ignorance, never crossed my mind" (*The Idea of Spatial Form* [Rutgers UP, 1991], xii). Frank's modesty is admirable, but the sentence feels very much like the kind of thing one said in 1991 that one did not say in 1945, when the atmospherics for syncretic work were quite different. Compare with the final sentence of the original essay: "And it is this timeless world of myth forming the content of so much of modern literature, that finds its appropriate aesthetic expression in spatial form" (64), which seems both "abstract" and "theoretical," and reaches well beyond the confines of "a particular work."

of the syncretic impulse means that the critical adventures of recent decades have yet to be significantly mined for their potential contributions to large-scale literary projects of the nomothetic type.

For now, in this more limited frame, some initial propositions. First, that worldedness, the world-oriented force of any given work of art, is an aesthetic effect that emerges only at certain scales of the work itself (and hence of the analysis of works). And second, that we can move toward a more systematic (if nonetheless still impressionistic and incomplete) sense of what worldedness means if we remark some particular *modes* or *variables* of its production.

Where in the work does worldedness emerge? It is perhaps easiest to imagine worlds at large scales, or ones that genre has already named: the novel, the oeuvre, the poem. But a sentence in a novel, a word in a poem, a look, an exclamation, or a punctuation mark can become worlds if read as formal totalities of their own, if attended to and conceived, like Blake's grain of sand, in a world-oriented way. This suggests that aesthetic worlds emerge in some significant symbiosis with a predetermined notion of the total form of the work, and the labor of the critic to find it. The critic helps make the work a world by recognizing it as a work; but the work also labors under the aegis of its own totality, and marks itself in ways that make its worldedness enticing to the critic. That is why Nancy suggests that the unity shared by the work and the world originates in the fact that "the reciprocity between 'world' and 'art' is constitutive of both."[2]

As for the oeuvre, whose unity essentially amounts to the establishment of another "work" over and above the individual works that make it up, it usually stems from the labor of a single artist. But we can also talk about oeuvre-worlds created by a number of different artists, as when the fantastic worlds of J. R. R. Tolkien

2 Jean-Luc Nancy, *The Creation of the World; or, Globalization*, trans. François Raffoul and David Pettigrew (SUNY P, 2007), 42.

or Gene Roddenberry become sites for the production of a wide variety of works, authorized and unauthorized, by any number of authors (including fans) drawn to the representational and narrative possibilities they hold in store. Legitimate new works of this type combine the original world's character-system and settings with the rules of its original genre.[3] Creating a work that belongs to an existing world means adopting its major characters, and its diegetic and extradiegetic rules, including its laws of narrative probability and its claimed relation to actual history. These rules collectively amount to the physics governing the most basic properties of the diegesis.

But how, exactly? It is good to know that worldedness occurs largely at the scale of the work or the collection of works that itself establishes a higher-order "totality of meaning," but how does it so occur?[4] Worldedness emerges most often from the collective expression—or *im*pression—of the work as a whole, as a function of all the rules that govern what the work does not include as well as what the work includes *without* mentioning it. World-creation happens consciously, but also in the ideological "unconscious" of the work, not as an expression of what the work does not know, but of what it knows most deeply, and thus says least: world is a "proliferation of intentionlessness."[5] From this perspective any aesthetic world is also an epistemological engine: a mechanism for the generation and exhibition of knowledge about itself as a totality. That knowledge will be full of gaps and silences, will include blanks and

---

3 A modernist novel starring Tintin, Captain Haddock, and Snowy establishes a world quite different from the one in the Hergé comics, and violates the compact whereby recognizable characters carry their world-rules with them. See, for instance, Frederic Tuten's *Tintin in the New World: A Romance* (William Morrow, 1993), whose Amazon reviewers spend most of their time angrily warning other Tintin fans away from the book.

4 The phrase "totality of meaning" is from Nancy, *Creation of the World*, 41.

5 Timothy Bewes, "Reading with the Grain: A New World in Literary Criticism," *differences* 21.5 (2010): 17.

refusals. Together these constitute the conversance of a world, its knowing relation to its own world-structure.

***

One slightly odd effect of this attention to the most basic forms of the ideological intentionlessness of the artwork, to the physics governing its production, will be that on more than one occasion what I have to say about a single work of art or type of work later on will seem simply to recapitulate something everyone already knows.

The world of the Symbolist poem, for instance, is most easily understood as a set of relations inside its representational, diegetic space, in which one or more mimetic referents (swans, vowels, forests) acquire a paradiegetic significance all out of proportion with their natural or material importance, a significance that unites the natural reference with its Symbolic counterpart (color, freedom, anagnorisis) while leaving the referent intact in the diegesis. If all one ends up saying about the "world" of a Symbolist poem is that it does all the things we already know Symbolist poems do, what exactly is the use of using the word *world* to describe it? Why not just say what a Symbolist poem does and be done with it?

My response: that part of the problem is that the people who describe Symbolist poems do not have, usually, much to say to the people who describe novels, epic theater, or such non-Western forms as *yuefu* poetry, the *monogatari*, or the *ghazal*. Because "worldedness" as an aesthetic concept applies broadly across the field of imaginative production (and includes, as I suggest later on, such obviously nonfictional but very much world-creating works as the concept of globalization or the paranoid style), it allows for comparative work across nation, language, genre, and time in ways that many of our contemporary concepts ("the Symbolist poem," or even "modernism") do not. "World" adds something to the analysis of the Symbolist poem by putting it in a context in which one of its major aesthetic and social functions can be compared with those of other works of art.

Second, the concept of the "world" as applied to a work of art serves a unifying purpose by emphasizing the total function—the totality of meaning—of the work. It focuses attention on how the various elements of the work create a dialectically or systemically organized whole (featuring, to be sure, holes). This methodological preference for the organization of parts into a whole, and thus for the analysis of structures and relations, stems from a belief that "the knowledge of empirical facts remains abstract and superficial as long as it has not been concretized by its integration into a whole that will allow one to move past partial and abstract phenomena in order to arrive at their *concrete essence*," as Lucien Goldmann once wrote.[6] For Goldmann as for others the "concrete essences" so approached were fundamentally social, and little is more social, I will argue in part 2, than the history of worldedness as it operates inside and outside the work of art.[7]

Third, the concept of the "aesthetic world," understood as a partial effect of a relation to the concept of "totality" organized by existing ideas of the *actual* world, allows us to recognize the long-standing relation between literature and the cosmological imagination, which extends back into the farthest reaches of human myth and human literature. This is so especially if we understand the "as such" of worldedness to include not only the concept of totality but

6 Lucien Goldmann, *Le Dieu caché: Étude sur la vision tragique dans les* Pensées *de Pascal et dans le théâtre de Racine* (Gallimard, 1959), 16, my translation.

7 The recourse to Goldmann reflects my interest in what Martin Jay has called Goldmann's "non-normative" use of the word *totality*, which (he writes) "stems from a methodological insistence that adequate understanding of complex phenomena can follow only from an appreciation of their relational integrity" (Jay, *Marxism and Totality: The Adventures of a Concept from Lukács to Habermas* [U of California P, 1984], 23–24). To which I would add: and the degree to which that integrity operates in a larger set of relations that includes disintegration, and thus refuses to, as Sartre said of Lukács, "liquidate the particularity" (cited in Jay, *Marxism and Totality*, 349).

also the notion of a human life and human presence in the historical world. As much is suggested by the word's etymology in English: a pairing of the Germanic *wer-*, meaning "man," and the Latinate *-ald*, "age" (via *altus*), hence, "age of man."[8] This grouping places at the center of the idea of world a notion of human activity and experience that ties the concept firmly to the self-conceptualizing, self-realizing activity of the species: philosophy and history, in all their forms.

For these reasons it seems to me that the concept of aesthetic worldedness is worth pursuing, even when it at times reconfirms a general impression that most people already had about Symbolist poetry, epic theater, *Gargantua and Pantagruel*, and so on. Because of the scale at which aesthetic worlds emerge, the value of thinking them lies not always in what they tell us about single works or single movements (about which we already know a great deal) but in the ways they allow us to compare works or movements to one another. It is a matter of focusing, as with an electron microscope, on the single depth plane of the cell wall—and of knowing that in any such focus the activity of the organelles does not, because unseen, cease to occur. This shift to a higher depth-plane, the focus at the world-scale on the conceptual wholes and "concrete essence" of the literary work as a social phenomenon, allows for the larger comparative structure I establish later on, where something new will, in fact, make an appearance.

8 The disheveled pairing of German and Latin makes "world" an odd match for the Latin *mundus*, whose meanings of pure, neat, and orderly, through "association with the Greek *cosmos* whose sense of harmony and order it translates ... becomes world and even universe," as Djelal Kadir has noted ("Old World, New World, Next World." Talk given at the American Comparative Literature Association conference, Cambridge, Mass., March 27, 2009). Things get even messier if we begin to think about the important differences between terms like "world," "planet," "globe," "Earth," "universe," and "cosmos," even in a single language, and then again if we go on to other languages, contrasting 世界 *shijie* and 天下 *tianxia* in Chinese, for instance. To write a comparative history of these concepts would be, indirectly, to write a history of totality as an effect of human life.

Chapter 5

Aspects of Worldedness

A world is conversant with itself. Is it possible to describe the impressionistic sense one has of any given aesthetic world as the product of a set of specific features of the world itself, as though they were variables or modes of that conversance?

Yes, more or less. Worldedness emerges as the unconscious of the work, as the establishing framework for the unmentioned rules that constitute the work as a total whole (that is, as a work at all), minimally through the mechanisms I list below. I have not attempted to create an exhaustive system. The spirit of this book is one of invention, discovery, and, in some cases, collocation or retrieval—several of the mechanisms, as you will see, extend long-standing concepts in literary criticism. My aim is to open up a general plane of description and analysis, one that would draw together a number of different forms of analysis to help us figure out how to talk about the "world" of the work. Such a capacity could reflect, in turn, the imaginative history of the world as a figure and ground for social life and historical time, and thereby highlight the vital importance of the history of art as a form of global imagination on par with (and with much to offer to) existing paradigms of world history, globalization, and so on.

All that must wait, however, for a minimal laying-out of some variables or mechanisms of world-production in literature, six of which I describe below.

AMPLITUDE

One of the best-known instances of twentieth-century literary criticism, the chapter "Odysseus' Scar" in Erich Auerbach's *Mimesis*, describes differences between a scene in Homer and the biblical episode of Abraham and Isaac.[1] In Auerbach's hands, the Greek and the Hebrew styles become "basic types" of literary representation: "on the one hand fully externalized description, uniform illumination, uninterrupted connection, free expression ... on the other hand, certain parts brought into high relief, others left obscure, abruptness, suggestive influence of the unexpressed, 'background' quality" (23). The movement between these types, the crossing and recrossing of the conceptual gap they establish, tell the story of the representation of reality in Western literature.

Auerbach's great contribution is to conceptualize and name representational ground. In his analysis, the Homeric episode is "scrupulously externalized," "clearly outlined, brightly and uniformly illuminated" (3), the style leaving "nothing which it mentions half in darkness and unexternalized" (5). Everything is there for the reader; the characters express their thoughts clearly and openly; the meaning of the scene in terms of the larger narrative appears sharply; and the long-forgotten episode of Odysseus's acquiring a scar on his foot appears in the same picture plane as the foot washing happening in the narrative present.

Abraham, by contrast, speaks to a God who is not in the immediate diegetic frame: "if we conceive of Abraham in the foreground, ... God is not there too: Abraham's words are directed toward the depths of the picture or upward, but in any case the undetermined,

---

1 Erich Auerbach, *Mimesis: The Representation of Reality in Western Literature*, trans. Willard Trask (Princeton UP, 2003). Further references in the text.

dark place from which the voice comes to him is not in the foreground" (9). The journey that follows the conversation, "like a silent
progress through the indeterminate and the contingent," appears
"like a blank duration between what has passed and what lies
ahead" (10): three days in which Abraham travels with Isaac to the
site of sacrifice, about which the text remains silent. The characters,
likewise, are taciturn: "their speech does not serve, as does speech
in Homer, to manifest, to externalize thoughts—on the contrary,
it serves to indicate thoughts which remain unexpressed," including the thought of God, who has tasked Abraham with the sacrifice
of his son but left his "motives and his purpose unexpressed" (11).
From the textual habits of the biblical writer Auerbach develops a
theory of narrative "background," which becomes in his hands not
merely a feature of the location within the story plane, but also a
mark of psychological depth and complexity (12), of biographical
or geographical history (13), of the possibility of and provocation
toward interpretation (13–14), and of an orientation toward "reality," since the biblical text, "far from seeking, like Homer, merely to
make us forget our own reality for a few hours, ... seeks to overcome
our reality: we are to fit our own life into its world, feel ourselves to
be elements in its structure of universal history" (15).

Let us put those last two possibilities—provocation to interpretation and orientation toward reality—aside for the moment. Both
extend the diegetic force of the relation between foreground and
background beyond the aesthetic world proper. They are, in short,
interpretations of the *historical significance* of a set of aesthetic practices, and not simply a description of those practices.

This excision permits a working definition of aesthetic amplitude, which refers to the relative spread of narrative attention across
the diegesis, and particularly of the distribution of that attention
relative to the narrative importance of any given object in diegetic
space. By "attention" I mean the degree to which any work can mark

as privileged some of its aspects by spending more time or space on them than on others, or by surrounding them with the marks of aesthetic interest appropriate to the formal regime to which the work of art belongs—placing them centrally in a frame, making them protagonists, describing them at length or illustrating them in detail, associating them with privileged paratexts (titles or epigraphs) or formal features (rhymes or soliloquies), accompanying them with shifts in discursive or figurative register, and so on. Attention spread equally among all parts of the diegesis produces, as Auerbach notes, a strong sense of total foregroundedness, which is, in effect, the mark of *zero amplitude*—a very small or even nonexistent gap between the foreground and background material. Attention unequally spread produces a gap between foreground and background, and attention very unequally spread leads to the sensation of mystery and wonder that permeates the twenty-second chapter of the book of Genesis.

It is not simply a case, therefore, of a difference between texts that are "all" foreground, as is the Homer in Auerbach's reading, and ones that leave things largely unexpressed. The Abraham narrative has foreground, but the significance of what it foregrounds is a product, formally speaking, of what the story leaves in the background. Likewise we might say that the Homeric episode presents not so much an instance of pure foreground as one in which foreground and background barely differentiate themselves. The meaning of characters or episodes in such a collapsed diegetic plane will not stem from differences in amplitude, but from other aspects of the work's progress. To be sure, some things *are* foregrounded in Homer: the major characters and episodes, the lives of certain types of people, and certain kinds of activity. But the material that is absent from the Homeric narrative—the quotidian or ordinary activity of daily life led by people unconnected to heroic history, among other things—does not register as absent in the text; and when people from the largely ignored orders of life do appear, as for instance Odysseus's old housekeeper Euryclea, they speak and act in exactly the same narrative register as the text's other characters. These gaps or absences, which might otherwise produce a sense of diegetic or characterological depth by populating the Homeric world with markers of stories the *Odyssey* does not tell or social spaces it leaves unaddressed, do not create any major stylistic or narrative effects. The result is a text whose surface defines a world that evinces no awareness of its incompleteness, but which rests in total comfort in relation to the adequacy of the narrative to the story and the telling to the diegesis.[2]

The book of Genesis and the *Odyssey* do not display only possible forms of world-constructing amplitude. Variations in amplitude occur between genres—the novel does not have the same balance as the romance, the sitcom as the procedural drama—as well as inside them. In a more contemporary context, one might remark that among the many differences between two of the major long-form American television dramas of the George W. Bush era, *The Wire* and *Battlestar Galactica*, is the fact that the enormous gap between background and foreground that created the tragic, inexorable mood of the former was so comparatively collapsed in the latter—and this despite the fact that of the two it was *Battlestar* that most insistently placed a sense of theological mystery and epic wonder at the center of its long-arc plot.

When amplitude refers to the structure of diegetic space, the balance between foreground and background as articulated by the distribution of aesthetic attention and information, one might think of it as operating on the z-axis of a three-dimensional graph (near to far); when it operates on the structure of diegetic time, on the

---

2 Compare this comfort to the feeling produced by the first half of Georges Perec's *Les choses*, in which a nearly zero degree of amplitude (far from usual in 1965) creates, instead, a sense of suffocation and dread.

x-axis (left to right). X-axis amplitude, a feature of narrative in the diegesis, stems from the appearance of *significant* temporal gaps or spaces in the aesthetic world—significant insofar as their exclusion from the diegesis is marked as an exclusion, and creates the same sense of absence or mystery in diegetic space as does the "location" of God's voice in Genesis.[3] Amplitudinal norms change over time: by the middle of the twentieth century a certain amount of unfilled x-axis amplitude becomes an aspect of the expectations of realism, as we see in André Bazin's comments on the films of Vittorio De Sica and Roberto Rossellini: "The empty gaps, the white spaces, the parts of the event that we are not given, are themselves of a concrete nature: stones which are missing from the building. It is the same in life: we do not know everything that happens to others."[4]

One might easily add to this pair a number of other dimensions of amplitude, including the social (distance covered by the highest to lowest arena of social action); the affective (gap between the most intensely and least intensely felt emotions); the psychological (relative "depth" of the internal life-worlds of the characters, their motivations, etc.); or the epistemological (the mysteries of Genesis vs. the clarities of Homer). One might also consider discussing metadiegetic amplitude (on the metadiegetic, see below). All of these together might constitute a total and generally describable single level of amplitude of the diegetic space. Or they might contradict one another sufficiently to prevent blanket statements, which would also be interesting.

3 The text's silence on the subject of the three days' walk is, from this perspective, an instance of horizontal rather than vertical amplitude, while the difference in the type of information it provides regarding God and Abraham, respectively, is one of vertical amplitude.

4 André Bazin, "De Sica: Metteur en Scène," in *What Is Cinema?* 2 vols. (U of California P, 1971), 2:66. I came across these lines in Jason McGrath, *Postsocialist Modernity: Chinese Cinema, Literature, and Criticism in the Market Age* (Stanford UP, 2008), 151.

Amplitude, then, describes the internal openness of the diegesis. A large gap between foreground and background, the presence of white spaces designated as "parts of the event," as in Genesis, create a world that is comparatively "spacious," a world whose visible/narrated aspects take up only a small portion of the total temporal, spatial, or epistemological volume opened up by the work. Homer by contrast is low amplitude and therefore "dense": the available life-space is essentially filled by the events and characters of the diegesis.[5] To read one of these approaches as more realistic than the other (as Auerbach does, following the line of development of European literature through to the modern novel) is to hold reality too steady. Surely, instead, the general development of literary norms toward the average amplitude that obtains in the contemporary novel reflects not a progressive discovery of the correct mechanisms for representing reality (a reality that has been there, like oxygen or quanta, all along), but a series of shifts in the theory of reality and of social space that are reflected, conceived, or imagined into possibility by the work of art.

COMPLETENESS

The philosophy of possible worlds declares that fictional worlds "are inherently incomplete.... Fictional entities are *logically* incomplete

---

5 Some of this feeling will also be a function of what Thomas Pavel has called a work's "referential density," the degree to which its available space or time (the square footage of its performance space, the hours of a film, the pages of a book or lines of a poem) feels empty or full, small or large. A ten-page essay on the Boston Tea Party does not, Pavel remarks, produce the same relative world-effects as a 1,500-page novel on the same subject (*Fictional Worlds* [Harvard UP, 1986], 101–2). But density can also be a feature of the arrangement of objects in the diegesis: Jules Verne, writes Roland Barthes, "had an obsession for plenitude: he never stopped putting a last touch to the world and furnishing it, making it full with an egg-like fullness" (Barthes, *Mythologies*, trans. Annette Lavers [Hill and Wang, 1972], 65).

because many conceivable statements about a fictional entity are undecidable," and "semantically *incomplete* because, being constructed by language, characteristics and relations of the fictional object cannot be specified in every detail."[6] So Ruth Ronen, describing the standard position. Call this the "price of apples" problem: what is the price of apples in the London of Dickens's *Oliver Twist*? We can never know, whereas for apples in 1837 London we at least presumably could find out. That's the difference between completeness (a feature of the actual world) and incompleteness.

Because all literary worlds are incomplete in this sense (and there is not much satisfaction in going around pointing it out over and over), we can focus on the way a given text manages incompleteness—whether it, for instance, assumes it, dramatizes it, ignores it, and so on. A work's relation (usually rhetorical or narratological) to the problem of incompleteness constitutes another variable in its world-orientedness. When Calogrenant in Chrétien de Troyes's *Yvain* comes upon a road "leading to the right, straight through a dense forest," Auerbach notes that the direction of the turn has no relation to terrestrial topography: "It must have an ethical signification. Apparently it is the 'right way' which Calogrenant discovered" (128–29). Symbolic significance trumps realistic necessity, a fact that governs the world of this late twelfth-century romance, as Auerbach goes on to suggest. Did the road "actually" turn right? The text does not care. Nor does it care, as might a novel, to suggest that there were any other turns on the road—that Calogrenant's decision to take *this* turn owed anything to the possibility of turning elsewhere. He has arrived at the right turn, and he turns rightly. The possibility of doing otherwise does not occur to him; nor does it occur to the fiction to suggest that it might have. Is there a turn in that forest? Is there even a forest "there," that is, "there" in some

6 Ruth Ronen, *Possible Worlds in Literary Theory* (Cambridge UP, 1994), 114.

terrestrial geography that we might identify? No. And don't bother asking about the price of apples.

In the novel, by contrast, the price of apples is perfectly "knowable," even though we cannot know it certainly. Unless that price acquires a special kind of narrative significance, it is, the reader can safely assume, whatever the price of apples was in the setting of the novel during those years; or it is whatever price of apples is appropriate to the general economy of the fictional place in question, which would only be worth mentioning if it were in fact somehow surprising or important, relative either to the needs of the fiction, or to the norm of the actual world of an expected ideal reader. Both solutions are good enough that average readers of Dickens, like average readers of Chrétien de Troyes, do not trouble themselves over apple prices. The two texts resolve the "problem" of incompleteness differently, and these differences help define, among other things, the differences between the worlds of medieval romance and the nineteenth-century English novel.

We find an example of the blending of those differences, somewhat tellingly, in the opening lines of Sir Walter Scott's *Ivanhoe* (1819): "In that pleasant district of merry England which is watered by the river Don, *there extended in ancient times* a large forest, covering the greater part of the beautiful hills and valleys which lie between Sheffield and the pleasant town of Doncaster."[7] Though Scott's forest (like his "merry" England) is no less symbolic than Chrétien's, its continuity with the present and its location in a named and verifiable geography guarantees, at least theoretically, its independence from the needs of fiction, and generates a wholly modern sense of completeness.[8]

---

7 Scott, *Ivanhoe* (Oxford UP, 1996), 1, my emphasis.

8 And though *Ivanhoe* makes the most of its geographic realism, its landscapes are not fully immune to the needs of story. When the Black Knight's purpose is "baffled by the devious paths through which he rode," the adjective "devious," whose whole purpose is to delay the Black Knight and to cause him to seek out a place in the West Riding of Yorkshire to spend the night, is a sign that geography has been subordinated to plot (and thus of a

Given those differences, can we therefore agree that "whatever the rhetoric of a literary text, unless explicitly stated otherwise, a completeness of the [literary] universe is always assumed"?[9] Not really. Consider Homer. You can't tell the Greek bard who comes to your village to recite parts of the *Odyssey* that just last week you heard another bard tell part of the same story, but that the *first* bard said that Ulysses was in Crete in the spring, and everyone *knows* it only takes twenty days to sail from Knossos to Argos, and so there's *no way* that Ulysses could have been in Argos when the second bard says he was. It's not that saying something like that would be annoying (though it would). It's that it would simply not make sense to the bard or to anyone else, because the Homeric world does not "assume" or generate completeness in the same way the novel does.

As the historicism of Scott's English forest suggests, completeness in narrative has a strong temporal dimension, since it refers not only to the knowledge of facts like apple prices but also to the ongoing existence of fictional objects that move out of the immediate frame of narrative or descriptive attention. Novels in the realist tradition have long played with this dimension, asserting the existence of their characters beyond the closing of the fiction without resorting to the formulaic structures (happily ever after, etc.) that the fairy tale used to accomplish, without much realism, a similar task. "What happens to Leopold Bloom on June 17, 1904" is not knowable, and this is as much a mark of Joyce's commitment to the realist tradition as anything else. But it would be wrong to imagine that the novel wished its readers to believe that Bloom ceased to exist. For

more "medieval" orientation toward the complete). Though geography rarely functions in the medieval romance as a marker of the kind of geographic and independently verifiable completeness with which we associate modern fiction, a romance like Malory's *Morte d'Arthur* may generate a certain social completeness by varying the minority and majority of its characters (a habit that falls under the analysis of character-system, discussed shortly).

9 Ronen, *Possible Worlds*, 140.

evidence take the limited history of the "Elijah is coming" throwaway that Bloom drops into the Liffey. *Ulysses* is almost obsessively
concerned—in a manner far beyond anything in Dickens, which
reserves its intensities for narratively important objects—with
tracking the flier's movements, noting its progress out to sea from
a perspective that does not belong to any of the novel's characters.
These observations, focalized through the novel's most privileged
narratorial position,[10] provide details whose function is to insist on
the novel's hyperrealistic temporal command over the continued
existence of all its diegetic objects, even when those objects seem,
as does the throwaway, to be largely devoid of narrative significance. At its limit, in the complete novel, "far from everything [in
the world] is mentioned in the novel itself, but the compact wholeness of the real world is sensed in each of its images; it is precisely in
this world that each image lives and acquires its form."[11]

The irony of these kinds of details is, as Roland Barthes has
noted, that their insignificance becomes, as a result, so very significant: in order to indicate to the reader that the diegesis is *generally* complete, one must instantiate the general assertion in specific
objects that, having been mentioned, can never achieve the zero-
degree of significance that would allow them actually to *be* the evidence they, instead, *indicate*.[12] The mere fact of existing gives them

10 Which Hugh Kenner calls "the Arranger" in *Ulysses*, rev. ed. (Johns Hopkins UP,
1987), 61–71.

11 Mikhail Bakhtin, "The *Bildungsroman* and Its Significance in the History of
Realism: Toward a Historical Typology of the Novel," in *Speech Genres and Other Late
Essays*, trans. Vern W. McGee, ed. Caryl Emerson and Michael Holquist (U of Texas P,
1986), 46.

12 Roland Barthes, "The Reality Effect," in *The Rustle of Language*, trans. Richard
Howard (U of California P, 1989), 142. Consider in this context Francis Jeffrey, writing in
1804: "With Richardson we slip, invisible, into the domestic privacy of characters, and see
every thing that is said and done among them, whether it be interesting or otherwise" (cited
in Ian Watt, *The Rise of the Novel: Studies in Defoe, Richardson, and Fielding* (U of California
P, 1957), 175). With that last clause we see the mark of a certain approach to completeness,
which consists in placing among the narratively relevant or representationally curious

more than no significance, though their major goal is to signify their own insignificance and thus to both (A) indicate the completeness of the diegetic world, and (B) establish a relative baseline against which both amplitude and narrative density can be measured.[13] Having followed it beyond the limits of Dublin proper, the reader can rest assured that whatever happens to Bloom on June 17, the throwaway, at least, will continue to do what real pieces of paper thrown into real rivers do, and for just as long as real pieces of paper do it.[14]

The continued existence of imaginary objects beyond their immediate apprehension by a living audience is known among users of contemporary online virtual worlds as "persistence." The term describes the fact that such worlds, unlike the worlds of single-player video games like *Pac-Man* or *Doom*, continue to exist when the individual player stops playing. History in such worlds is not a function of the attention of any single player, nor is it necessarily the function of the combined attention of all players. Instead it results from the arrangement of the game-space's most basic ludic structure, which mimics the real world by disconnecting narrative and descriptive viability from any single or collective act of perception. Continuity without human presence is thus part of the nature of such games, which could theoretically run on servers long after the

aspects of the diegesis material whose major function is to be essentially *uninteresting*—except insofar as they are, of course, precisely that.

13 As for the throwaway, *Ulysses* lards it with symbolic force: the horse *Throwaway* wins the Gold Cup, leading to all sorts of consequences for Bloom, and the phrase "Elijah is coming" is full of implications for Bloom and for Stephen. But none of these require the passage of a piece of paper down the Liffey to be so precisely tracked.

14 Or consider, in this same context, the water flowing to Bloom's home "from Roundwood reservoir in county Wicklow of a cubic capacity of 2,400 million gallons, percolating through a subterranean aqueduct of filter mains of single and double pipeage," described in the novel's penultimate chapter, which had appeared to the reader during Bloom's morning trip to the bathhouse as a "clean trough of water" (James Joyce, *Ulysses* [Vintage International, 1990], 86. I am grateful to Ali Frauman for the example).

extinction of the human race—though their world history in that carefree age would be, I imagine, severely curtailed.

In individual works that represent time an effect similar to that of persistent online worlds can be obtained by gestures like Joyce's tracking of the Elijah throwaway.[15] Just as efficient and more striking, however, is the manner in which the gap between individual works set in the same world, or even individual chapters in the same work, creates a strong sense of the "persistence" of elements of the diegesis beyond the immediate attention of the controlling narrative. Certain kinds of incompleteness thus matter as much to worldedness as efforts at total completeness. While the latter may well assure us of the total solidity and answerability of the work-world (as in some poetic lipograms in Christian Bök's *Eunoia*), the former, by expanding horizontal amplitude, locate the events or actions of the diegesis firmly in a world whose incompleteness feels, as Bazin suggests, "the same as in life."[16] That undescribed, unnarrated events have occurred to Bianchon between the end of *Le Père Goriot* and the opening of *L'Interdiction* speaks more powerfully to his persistence (indeed, his life!) than any critical detail or description that actually appears in the novels themselves.[17] By

15 We must be careful to read any work's relation to persistence in relation to the aesthetic context of its moment. Watt warns against overreading the gaps and silences of *Moll Flanders*, on the theory that for Defoe "we must posit a kind of limited liability for narrative," since Defoe "did not keep his characters in mind when they were off the stage" (Watt, *Rise of the Novel*, 110–11). It is precisely the difference between Defoe's not keeping his characters "in mind" and Joyce's doing so that a variable like completeness attempts to register.

16 Auerbach, on the modernist novel's development of multiple perspectives on the same event: "These are the forms of order and interpretation which the modern writers here under discussion attempt to grasp in the random moment—not one order and one interpretation, but many, which may either be those of different persons or of the same person at different times; so that overlapping, complementing, and contradiction yield something that we might call *a synthesized cosmic view* or at least a challenge to the readers' will to interpretive synthesis" (*Mimesis*, 549, my emphasis).

17 The gap between novels opens up a sense of completeness that would only be violated were it to be revealed that the Bianchon of the later work has nothing to do, despite all

High Amplitude / High Completeness Joyce, *Ulysses*	High Amplitude / Low Completeness *Genesis*
Low Amplitude / High Completeness Perec, *Les choses*	Low Amplitude / Low Completeness *The 1980s sitcom*

Figure 1.1. Quadrant for amplitude and completeness

contrast to Balzac's characters, the personages in Genesis are like puppets taken down from a shelf to play. Their tale complete, they fall into a silence deeper than death. That silence ends when, out of some new necessity, the story picks up their strings and makes them dance again. In this way they resemble the characters of the classic television sitcom.[18]

METADIEGETIC STRUCTURE

Having earlier hived off the question of interpretation from Auerbach's concept of foreground and background, we can now address the call to interpretation as a separate effect of aesthetic worldedness, one that determines how any given object, character, or event in the diegesis signifies metadiegetically, at a level indirectly or only partially subject to diegetic action.[19] Objects, events,

the similarities, with the Bianchon of the former—but that would make for a very different world indeed.

18 The effort to generate persistence, and the sense of simultaneity that so often accompanies it (especially when, as in the contemporary thriller or the epistolary fiction, alternating chapters focus on different characters entirely), generates the sense of homogeneous, empty time that Benedict Anderson, reading Walter Benjamin, associated so strongly with the rise of nationalism, in *Imagined Communities: Reflections on the Origin and Spread of Nationalism*, rev. ed. (Verso, 2006).

19 And indeed in some cases may be "prior" to it, since interpretive content (the meaning of a dream, for instance) can function inside a narrative as the causal origin of its own literal manifestation. This difficult temporal relation between the "natural" and

characters, or formal features that signify intensely at the metadiegetic level (that call out, in some sense, for interpretation) can be distributed quite differently. Their distribution relative to the size (or length, in pages, or time) of the diegesis as a whole will determine the *metadiegetic structure* of a given aesthetic world, or of any given moment in it.

Preliminarily—the list is indicative, not complete—let us describe three types of metadiegetic structure. Because I am trying to describe aesthetic world-space, these types focus on their appearances in the diegesis, rather than on their distribution in the material and chronological unfolding of the *text*.[20] Call the types figural, narrative, and logical.[21]

In the figural, a diegetic object (character, space, moment, event) is marked off as an especially intense site of interpretive force, one whose effects resonate *beyond* the immediate diegetic sphere. The relation between object and its metadiegetic meaning differs depending on the type of figuration. The latter's traditional arrangements include allegory, symbol, and metaphor, but may be extended

"interpreted" meaning of any given sign (what Freud called the "manifest" and the "latent" content of the dream-work) suggests that the "meta" in "metadiegetic" here and elsewhere responds largely to the conventional belief that the literal precedes the metaphorical (in either causal, that is, temporal terms, or in the arrangement of "priorities" that we conceive as hierarchical [as in allegory] or systematic [as in an analysis that attributes a given superstructure to a base of some kind]).

20 As Roland Barthes does in *S/Z*, trans. Richard Miller (Hill and Wang, 1974). *S/Z* describes the text's unfolding over time, diachronically, the experience of the reader's engagement with the world (this is the general realm of narratology, the study of the *narration* of the story in the discourse). Here I am interested in the effects of the aesthetic world considered not as the subject of expression (*narration* in the fictional case) but as a represented object, and thus with its synchronic "existence" insofar as such a thing can exist alongside, or outside, its being expressed. Hence the emphasis on diegesis.

21 The list could be expanded by anyone who knows more than I do about anything. In thinking metadiegesis in film, for instance, one would want to consider something like the kinesthetic shocks Mark Hansen finds theorized in Walter Benjamin, which would allow us to talk about the effects of both sound and image that operate independently (though always in relation to) the fields of narrative, symbol, or allegory (Hansen, *Embodying Technesis: Technology Beyond Writing* [Michigan UP, 2000]).

to include any figure that encodes a relation between two levels of diegetic "reality" (the fetish, the myth, the totem, the emblem, and so on).[22] Each such figure establishes a different relation between the diegetic object and its metadiegetic significance. These differences powerfully shape the world of the artwork, either by adding a totally new dimension that dominates and to some extent obviates or overwhelms the diegesis (allegory), by adding a new dimension that parallels and sustains it (symbol), or by establishing, as in *figura*, a taut historical resonance between the sign and its signifieds.[23] The figural is from this perspective also a theory of the literal; an arrangement of relations between the "plain" and the "significant," and thus an arrangement of the physics of diegetic meaning. The differences between a heavily allegorized world like that of *Vanity Fair* and a heavily symbolized one, as in Octave Mirbeau's 1899 *Le Jardin des supplices*, represent a substantive difference in the structure and orientation of the aesthetic world, and a position on the nature of significance itself. Figural metadiegesis thus describes the modes of relationship assumed between sacred and profane space, in the religious life-world, or to the more general relationship between a primary referential layer and a secondary one (real Paris vs. Balzac's Paris; Sancho's windmills vs. Don Quijote's giants) governing the internal ontological structure of all made worlds—what Thomas Pavel calls the "salience" of fictional ontologies.[24]

22 Do these "magical" figures survive the advent of realism? Yes, but often in altered form. Realism re-encodes them as expressions of narrative-realistic outcomes: dreams, insanity, hallucinations, etc.

23 Consider in this context Tertullian's insistence on "literal and historical validity of the Old Testament," despite its role as a prefigurative anticipation of the New one: for him, "even where there was figural prophecy, the figure had just as much historical reality as what it prophesied" (Erich Auerbach, "Figura," in *Scenes from the Drama of European Literature* [U of Minnesota P, 1984], 30). My discussion of the figural mode is very much indebted to Auerbach's essay.

24 Pavel, *Fictional Worlds*, 54–64 passim.

Narrative metadiegesis describes the relation between the sub-objects of a given story (its characters, settings, episodes, and so on) and the larger story-structure in which they take part. Chekhov once noted that "if in Act 1 you have a pistol hanging on the wall, then it must fire in the last act."[25] This is among other things a formal theory of narrative metadiegetic necessity, in which the appearance of certain kinds of socially meaningful objects (guns, e.g.) must be accompanied by an equally important narrative significance. But a novel in which all the pistols "shoot," as it were, is quite a different novel than one littered with unfired revolvers. Realist fiction gives any number of examples of the latter practice, enough for Roland Barthes to describe realism's inclusion of the "useless" descriptive detail as a crucial component of the "reality effect." In such novels pistols that do not fire register nothing but their own being-thereness, indexing the novel's reportorial ambitions and the para-narrative amplitude of its diegetic space.[26] When postmodernism arrives, one of its responses to the Chekhovian demand is to include diegetic objects, or even events, that seem to carry no narrative significance at all, thereby frustrating the reader's expectations for the normal distribution of meaning across narrative space.

The logical mode of metadiegetic significance refers to the way the work articulates or layers over its diegetic events with a logical structure borrowed from some other, usually philosophical, sphere. For instance, as Andrew Plaks suggests, patterns of bipolar opposition in the Chinese novel frequently operate under a "central premise of ceaseless alternation" between terms, which eliminates "any

---

25 Donald Rayfield, *Anton Chekhov: A Life* (Northwestern UP, 2000), 203.

26 It may be the case that "narrative metadiegesis" could have a more generic name, something like formal or generic metadiegesis, which would allow it to refer to the degree to which any work of art can mark parts of itself as especially relevant to interpretation, by directing the audience's attention to those features most appropriate to the historical understanding of that work as a member of its aesthetic class (space or shape in sculpture, perspective or color in painting, rhythm or tone in music, and so on).

possibility of dialectical resolution." The effect of this pattern is to prevent a resolution of certain forms of narrative tension through either the final triumph of one or the other major terms, or their sublimation into a new stasis or order; more likely are modes of resolution that locate one pole "inside" the other (stillness within movement, e.g.).[27] On the basis of this example we may grasp the ways in which the diegesis may signify at the level of a world-physics whose rules may not be the subject of diegetic action. All tragedy is a meditation on tragedy, to be sure, but the rules governing the significance of any single feature of the tragic diegesis (the tragic flaw, e.g.) cannot be—except in metafiction—subjects of diegetic action. The concept of logical metadiegesis thus allows us to distinguish works along two lines: we may first identify some works as more heavily structured by some kind of external logic (dualism, tragedy, etc.) than others (which may be more figural); second, we may wish to distinguish among the *types* of external logic favored by certain periods, literary traditions, or genres. As much can be gathered from the comparison Plaks makes between the classical Chinese and European traditions, whose differences we might wish to be able to describe.

Any work or a genre will organize itself primarily around one or more types of metadiegetic significance (figural, logical, narrative, alone or in combination). Ian Watt observes such a difference at the level of genre when he argues that Defoe was England's first novelist. Though many of the elements that make Defoe's books novels appear in earlier Puritan fiction, Watt writes, "The significance of the characters and their actions [there] largely depends upon a transcendental scheme of things," because "their earthly reality is not the main object of the writer."[28] In Defoe by contrast the earthly

27 Andrew Plaks, "Conceptual Models in Chinese Narrative Theory," *Journal of Chinese Philosophy* 4.1 (1977): 36, 35.

28 Watt, *Rise of the Novel*, 80.

reality is the main thing the novels know and are interested in. His metadiegetic schema shifts radically along the figural-narrative axis, moving from an emphasis on the doubled-over, allegorical significance of the diegetic "ground," to a focus on the relations among objects of that ground, and thus on their narrative importance.

Metadiegetic structure thus allows us to discuss the ways a work assigns and distributes certain kinds of importance; the way that it articulates the forms of significance available in a total world-space (diegesis + metadiegesis). Differences in types of metadiegetic significance and the density of their distribution mark not only the labor of the fiction but also a theory of the world as among other things an arrangement of significances and relations, meagerly or generously distributed, and open (or not) to the possibility of communication among their levels. A society or a genre in which allegory dominates has, presumably, a different theory of the world (of the work) than one in which symbol or logic does; more pointedly, we can certainly discern, as Plaks does, that the orientation of Chinese fiction toward oscillating logical dualisms in the metadiegetic interpretive sphere has parallels in Chinese cosmology and philosophy, of which it is both an expression and a thinking through or beyond.[29] Representationally, and in terms consonant with the European experience of modernity, we might thus begin to imagine metadiegetic density as a way to figure what Max Weber would describe as the "enchantment" of the world—the degree to which, and how, the world contains the figural, narrative, or historical objects (miracles, turning points, heterotopias[30]) that make it

29 Another instance: while the Homeric and biblical texts differ in their degree of allegorical and symbolic density, their narrative density is more or less identical; though some objects matter more than others, to be sure, the topography that would graph the general distribution of such mattering remains, across each story, more or less flat. (In other words, neither narrative features many unfired revolvers; though even here one might observe that the biblical text has still fewer of those than the Homeric one.)

30 On heterotopias: the concept briefly developed by Michel Foucault in 1967 includes among its principles the claim that "the heterotopia is capable of juxtaposing in a

rationally or irrationally "magic" or significant, that generate in it multiple levels of signification whose relation cannot be reduced, as in an equation, to a single common denominator.[31]

CONNECTEDNESS

In *Graphs, Maps, Trees*, Franco Moretti maps the narrative geography of the five volumes of Mary Mitford's *Our Village*, showing how the social forces operating between 1824 and 1832 reproduce themselves in literary form. The concentric circles into which the novels arrange their episodes produce a "map of ideology emerging from a map of *mentalité*, emerging from the material substratum of the physical territory" of the village.[32]

On grounds like these one can easily oppose the village novel to globetrotting, cosmopolitan fiction, the adventure-driven

single real place several spaces, several sites that are in themselves incompatible." Examples include the theater, the cinema, and the garden; the latter is "the smallest parcel of the world and then it is the totality of the world." The distribution of these spaces is in effect a distribution of enchantment, a topography of distortion and possibility (Foucault, "Of Other Spaces [1967], Heterotopias," http://foucault.info/documents/heteroTopia/foucault.heteroTopia.en.html).

31 For the literary critic, everything is potentially significant: the text is saturated with meaning. But within a single text not every word or every sentence is saturated equally (at least not in general—and the work that was so evenly saturated would be making an argument of its own). Though in *S/Z* Barthes has something to say about every sentence of Balzac's "Sarrasine," he has more to say about some sentences (and some words) than others. A topographical map showing the number of words Barthes spends on each word of Balzac's would direct us to particular moments of density of significance, as would a similar map of, say, the accumulated scholarship on *Faust*, which collectively pays more attention to some sentences or episodes than others. (For the curious: Barthes divides the Balzac story into 561 lexias, which he analyzes for 200 pages in the English edition; the story itself covers 32.5 pages. Lexia 280 appears in the story 20 pages in—about 60 percent of the way through the story; its discussion appears 114 pages, or 57 percent of the way, into Barthes's analysis.)

32 Franco Moretti, *Graphs, Maps, Trees: Abstract Models for Literary History* (Verso, 2005), 42.

picaresque to the urban *Bildungsroman,* and so on. Along the way one will remark how much certain seemingly self-contained fictional places are punctuated, often with no narrative acknowledgment, by goods, people, or ideas that speak to the intensity of the connections between the local and the regional or the global—tea, coffee, or spices in any European novel after 1700, for instance. These are all markers of the work's relation to the world, just as the presence of felt hats, maps, and porcelain show, in the work of Johannes Vermeer, the artist confronting, alongside other seventeenth-century Europeans, "the idea of the world as an unbroken surface on which there is no place that cannot be reached, no place that is not implied by every other place, no event that belongs to any world but the one they now had to share."[33]

The idea of the world as an unbroken surface; a theory of a world infinitely connectable; works that register the fact and the possibilities of connection in diegetic space. Other representations give us diegetic worlds that are simply disconnected from that which does not take place in them—into which no rumor, no object, no event penetrates, or in which time passes (as it does in García Márquez's Macondo) at a rate that has nothing to do with the "outside"—if outside there be. Utopias, I have noted, are usually reached through quasi-metaphysical apertures (storms, wormholes, time machines, radically idealized political processes). You might compare the role such apertures play with the importance, for some fictions, of the door of the home. Here we have a model for a general relation of connectedness between diegetic spaces, one that applies as well to the travels of the narrative point of view in a novel as to the intensity of relations between two different parts of a picture plane, or to the structures created by the repetition of rhymes in a poem. In this

---

33 Timothy Brook, *Vermeer's Hat: The Seventeenth Century and the Dawn of the Global World* (Bloomsbury, 2008), 23.

sense connectedness also indicates a general field of transactability or exchange, the possibility of conversion or conversation across different "levels" of the diegesis—whether these be spatial, social, or epistemological. (For instance: works in which the interior psychological state of a character can be brought out into the open, manipulated, discussed, and changed, assume a basic transactability of interior and exterior, private and public, that does not govern, say, works in which moods, though they may exist, are simply not subject to the action of the plot. Here again a comparison between the novel and the romance is instructive.)

If we limit "connectedness" to the degree to which structures located at one level (or marked as one type) in the diegesis (protagonist, setting, and so on) relate to exteriors or interiors that swathe or puncture them—to describe, that is, relations between *divisions within a system*—then we can use "networkedness" to describe the collective intensity of relations between actors within a division.[34] Recent adventures in understanding the rules that govern networks and other complex systems have focused on the "laws of pure form" that determine their most important properties, leading Mark Buchanan to proclaim the discovery of "mathematical laws and meaningful patterns for the human world" that demonstrate the "natural" patterns of autopoietic efficiency—a claim echoed, though with substantially more political anxiety, by Manuel Castells in *The Rise of the Network Society*, and discussed in literature by Thomas LeClair's work on the systems novel.[35] Highly networked systems produce what the mathematicians call "small worlds," a phrase that

34 The distinction is loose, but usefully so: a given work's distribution of levels or types (separated by diegetic or formal barriers—social classes, or chapters), or its refusal to indulge in the production of levels, could be a further subject of analysis.

35 Mark Buchanan, *Nexus: Small Worlds and the Groundbreaking Science of Networks* (Norton, 2002), 12; Manuel Castells, *The Rise of the Network Society* (Blackwell, 1996); Thomas LeClair, *In the Loop: Don DeLillo and the Systems Novel* (U of Illinois, 1987).

reminds us, via Disney, that the imaginaries that govern science are no less literary than the ones that govern the aesthetic.

Networkedness in aesthetic worlds allows us to talk about the sense of diegetic world-space created by the village marketplace's selling of tea or a casual mention of an Oriental carpet, but also about how the world theorizes the set of relations among its various characters. Highly networked worlds are "small" not because of their spatial extension but because of their high interconnectivity; likewise referentially "small" spaces (houses, ships, rooms) can be "large" or disconnected worlds if action there creates diegetic effects only within the immediate sphere of its production—as is often the case in modern drama.[36] Likewise, we can observe changes in the diegetic *types* of networkedness in various novels. Contrast, for instance, the labor of the "leaden circles" of sound created by Virginia Woolf's Big Ben, the role of debt in Balzac, of family relationships in *Dream of the Red Chamber*, or of the Round Table in Arthurian romance. In each case a feature of the socioscape—the sound of a clock, the movement of capital, patriarchy, or the shape of a table—also serves as an important actor in narrative discourse, justifying, for instance, shifts in focalization from one character to another (internal in Woolf, external in Malory's *Morte d'Arthur*), or creating occasions for the emergence of new characters (long-lost cousins, secret purchasers of debts), which in turn drive new movements in the plot. Analyses of these types of networks, which would track not only the number of connections but their structure and hence mathematical nature, could require the aggregation of large amounts of data and their deployment and analysis according

---

36 Though consider Barthes on Verne: the ship "is ... the emblem of closure ... all the ships in Jules Verne are perfect cubby-holes, and the vastness of their circumnavigation [of the world, of the stars] further increases the bliss of their closure, the perfection of their inner humanity." The true opposite of Verne's *Nautilus* is, Barthes goes on to say, Rimbaud's drunken boat (Barthes, *Mythologies*, 66–67).

to mathematical principles; a limited vision of what such analysis might look like appears in work recently done by Moretti's Stanford-based Literature Lab.[37]

Connectedness and networkedness may be, as Alex Beecroft has suggested, partially a feature of the work's expected audience. Beecroft develops a typology of literary works as a function of their "political and economic environment," suggesting that literature produced within the framework of a local community differs in orientation (and style?) from that produced in cosmopolitan, national, or global frameworks.[38] Assuming Beecroft is willing to believe that works not only reflect such orientations, but conceive, refuse, or otherwise engage with them, such a model would allow critics to approach aesthetic worlds from the "outside," as it were, without presupposing that the field of address exerts a determining effect on the aesthetic sphere.

Connectedness and networkedness are features of the communicative structure of the aesthetic world. What transacts or

---

37 Franco Moretti, "Network Theory, Plot Analysis," at Stanford LitLab, litlab.stanford.edu/LiteraryLabPamphlet2.pdf, May 1, 2011, and in abbreviated form in *New Left Review* 68 (March–April 2011). The speculations Moretti makes about the role Horatio plays in *Hamlet*'s character-network, and the distinctions the network reveals between the court and the anti-court, seem to me to reveal the play's distribution of levels (what Moretti, who knows more about networks than I do, calls "network regions" [7]), and thus the utility of having a concept like "connectedness" to use in the analysis of diegetic worlds. That said, the conclusion to Moretti's essay—that network theory quickly reaches a limit beyond which a certain level of mathematical sophistication and network theory are necessary for further progress (or at least the hope of further progress)—confirms my sense that the intuitional qualities of the concepts I develop here make them more valuable *as tools to be used by many people*, and thus as open-source formations for future scholarship, discussion, and exchange, than at least some of the methods emerging from the more complex projects of Moretti's type, partly because those projects are currently only available to a tiny minority of literary scholars. It is of course possible that the kinds of work made possible by my more intuitionist categories will be limited in scope and applicability, and will thus be superseded by the new kinds of team-based analysis. We'll see.

38 Alex Beecroft, "World Literature without a Hyphen," *New Left Review* 54 (Nov.–Dec. 2008): 91. On the circulation of literary world-modes, see also Pavel, *Fictional Worlds*, 91–93.

transects the physical or represented spaces of the work, whether they be couplets, houses, or quadrants of a picture plane? Does communication happen across object-boundaries, between social structures or groups (formally, this is Auerbach's "separation of styles"), between people and things, or people and their environments? Does the work represent, formally or diegetically, a breakdown in communication—a failure to enact a desirable transaction (marriage, a sale, an understanding)? Is that breakdown resolved, and how? These are world-oriented questions if we consider that the mediation that permits communication itself acts on the nature of the world-structure, by placing all that is communicable on the same ontological plane, will reinforce an idea "of the world as an unbroken surface on which there is no place that cannot be reached, no place that is not implied by every other place," as in the world of the Vermeer painting. And one that does not, will not, at least not in the same way.

CHARACTER-SYSTEM

There is some overlap between well-recognized features of narrative discourse and aesthetic worldedness. Nowhere is this clearer than with the concepts of character-space and character-system developed by Alex Woloch in *The One vs. the Many*. In that work Woloch reads the total distribution of characters in a narrative system—their number, their relative importance to the plot, their role as "major" or "minor," their access to direct speech, to metacommentary, or to such privileged forms of narration as free indirect discourse or focalization—as a "socioformal" aspect of the novel's self-organization.[39] The contest for character-space, he shows,

39 Alex Woloch, *The One vs. the Many: Minor Characters and the Space of the Protagonist in the Novel* (Princeton UP, 2003), 17.

is among other things the realist novel's attempt to come to grips with the representability of a social whole so unevenly populated by people whose representational value in democratic politics is theoretically identical.

Character-system is a feature largely of narrative worldedness, one that measures the distribution of two very different resources. The first, invariably limited, simply involves the number of pages devoted to any character. The second, unlimited, involves characterological access to privileged narrative markers (the opportunity to have their point of view "shown," e.g.). Equal or unequal distributions of these forms of privilege effectively create an economy of representation, a field of contestation and social organization that represents—and *practices*—civil society in the modern democratic era. Character-systems become dynamic in the realist novel, Woloch suggests, because the forms of social privilege that had previously been more or less normatively and permanently determined have opened up to the possibility of mobility and change.

How, in dynamic social systems, to decide who is "major" and "minor" is something Chrétien de Troyes or Murasaki Shikibu never had to worry about, since in both *Yvain* and the *Tale of Genji* the question of characterological importance is answered by the distribution of importance in the society the fictions represent. Though, therefore, one of *The Tale of Genji*'s major social features is that none of its major characters is "ever alone," they are nonetheless alone all the time, in the sense that a medieval Japanese lady surrounded by three or four servants is not in the presence of any of any of her social or characterological equals.[40] Compare this to Don

40 Royall Tyler, introduction to *The Tale of Genji*, by Murasaki Shikibu, trans. Royall Tyler (Penguin, 2002), xix. But of course what makes *Genji* so like a novel (or: a novel) is that the servants do in fact become characters, that Genji himself has the odd and diegetically unique capacity for disrupting the socio-characterological system, which is why he is, in some respects, not quite human.

Quijote, who is similarly almost always with servants, but whose servants have become—and not just in a farcical manner appropriate to the premodern separation of styles—actual characters in the narrative!

Though character-system appears most strongly only in the age of the realist novel, can it count as a general feature of aesthetic worlds beyond the modern period? Yes, if only because it directs us to the degree that all works that represent human life constitute social wholes, and thus to the ways that the arrangement of personages in diegetic space reflects (and reflects on) the dynamism of the social sphere the diegesis represents. Here it is helpful to recall a sentence from the epigraph to Fredric Jameson's *The Political Unconscious*, a citation from Émile Durkheim: "the very concept of totality is but the abstract form of the concept of society: that whole which includes all things, that supreme class under which all other classes must be subsumed."[41] There is thus no concept of society that is not also a concept of the social *sphere*, and of a totality that is a world, theorizing human enworldedness by virtue of its very self-consolidation. Though societies are not worlds, character-system as a world-variable alerts us to the site of their theoretical and practical intersection, and allows the complexity and force appropriate to each to become more clearly visible.

DYNAMISM

Mikhail Bakhtin's "The *Bildungsroman* and Its Significance in the History of Realism" distinguishes subgenres of the novel on the basis of the hero's relation to historical time. The travel novel—the classical

41 Fredric Jameson, *The Political Unconscious: Narrative as a Socially Symbolic Act* (Cornell UP, 1981), 8.

naturalist wandering stories, the European picaresque—"enables the artist to develop and demonstrate the spatial and static social diversity of the world," in which "temporal categories are extremely poorly developed": though such novels are full of hours, next days, that nights, and so on, these immediate units do not compose a sociocultural whole. The novel of ordeal, Bakhtin writes, develops "psychological time," the time of the hero's transformation, which it sets against a surrounding world that becomes "a mere background for the hero ... a decoration, a setting." "The world is not capable of changing the hero; it only tests him; and the hero does not affect the world, he does not change its appearance," but "leaves every-thing in the world in its place." The biographical novel relies on "biographical time," which "cannot but be included in the longer process of historical, but embryonically historical, time"; its hero "is not tested, but strives for actual results" in the depicted world. "Because of the link with historical time and with the epoch," says Bakhtin, in the biographical novel "it becomes possible to reflect reality in a more profoundly realistic way."[42]

I shall have more to say about the words *reality* and *realistic* in that last sentence in the second part of this book. For now it suffices to note that Bakhtin's elaboration of the various relations between hero and time in the history of the novel lays open another face of aesthetic world-imagination: its inclusion of the various modali-ties and types of time, and its distribution of those forms of time in diegetic space and narrative action. Bakhtin elaborates this category to trace, as the essay's subtitle suggests, "a historical typology of the novel," following a developmental through-line from Rome to the European *Bildungsroman*. There, the arc of ever-increasing dynamic interaction between hero and historical time finds its endpoint in

---

42 Bakhtin, "The *Bildungsroman* and Its Significance in the History of Realism," 10–11, 15–16, 18. Further citations in the text.

Goethe, in whose novels "man's individual emergence is inseparably linked to historical emergence," in which the hero "emerges *along with the world* and he reflects the historical emergence of the world itself" (23). In Goethe the world no longer acts as background, an unchanging quantity, but becomes the stuff of transformation, revealing the "*necessary connections* between this past and the living present," and grasping "the *necessary place* of this past in the *unbroken line of historical development*" (33). The dynamic relation between historical and heroic time enacted in Goethe's novels of emergence, the fully "connected" interpenetrability and interplay of temporal background and narrative foreground—now neither "background" nor "foreground" in any pure sense—establishes, for Bakhtin, the great triumph of the post-Enlightenment perception of reality.[43]

The implications of that argument, like Bakhtin's ease with the terms "reality" and "realistic," will be reserved for part 2, so that here we can observe that the kinds of dynamism Bakhtin uses to elaborate the historical typology of the novel can be extended beyond the novel form, if not, perhaps, beyond narrative. Indeed, we can think through dynamism as a world-feature by remapping several of the categories developed so far onto time: amplitude, to describe the distance between temporal foreground and background; connectedness, to describe the relationships between levels; and completeness, to grasp time's extension in (and potentially beyond) the diegetic sphere. Bakhtin's typology of temporalities adds the reminder that such world-variables must be thought in relation to qualitatively different *types* of time, the biological or the biographical, for example, which in turn suggests that we may wish to develop (belatedly) an

43 As the use of "connected," "background," and "foreground" here suggests, the other variables may prove useful in elaborating the nature of dynamism, which remains its own variable because it draws attention not simply to the connectedness or location of a fiction's temporalities, but to the very *types* of temporality it organizes.

equally complex sense of the different types of *space*. You might imagine, on these grounds, that any given character, event, place, or object in a fiction appears within a sort of "penumbra of effective action," which determines the spatial and temporal range, and degree, of its possible influence on the diegetic world—an influence that potentially extends, in the case of characters, both outward (toward the world) and inward (toward the self); we might therefore speak of a psychological (internal) dynamism as well as a historical (external) one. The collection of these penumbras arranged in the diegesis establishes the work's dynamism in general, its general theory of the forms of interaction between the *activity* it contains and the immanent world-surface upon and through which that activity occurs.[44] The entire world-system of a given work will thus present its readers with a shifting mass of time- and space-relations that are best considered as parts of the spatio-temporal whole they constitute, in which a variety of types of space and time interact along the dimensions described by the variables outlined here. Elsewhere, and famously, Bakhtin named that whole the "chronotope," a term whose frequent use in his essay on the *Bildungsroman* coincides with, and occasionally substitutes for, the term "world."

* * *

These six variables—amplitude, completeness, metadiegetic structure, connectedness, character-system, and dynamism—apply differently to different types of work. They resonate most clearly when it comes to narrative (in poetry, film, drama, or prose), where the necessary arrangement of relations in space and time strongly

---

44 Someone like Don Quijote has a high degree of local transformational power, in the sense that he makes huge messes wherever he goes. But the places he has been return to their "normal" state almost immediately after he leaves; he also has no effect on the larger political or social structure of his world or, for that matter, on his own character. For something like the epic, or a Tom Clancy novel, things are quite different.

generates a sense of worldedness. But even in works that suspend either the spatial or the temporal dimension (some haikus, some photographs, some music) worlds nonetheless emerge, if nowhere other than in the internal amplitude or connectedness of the work, allowing us to describe the difference between Cage's 4'33" and an Atget photograph of a deserted street, or to compare the amplitude of the haiku (traversed by the metadiegetic lightning bolt that ties the referent to its symbolic echo) to that of the paranoid style in American politics (in which a similarly large gap between the seen and the unseen is inevitably traversed *step-by-step*, in a parody of ratiocination).

The variables interact, also, with features of the artwork that do not speak directly to worldedness. When Moretti asks, for instance, why the major Chinese novels tend to be so long, and to feature so many characters, he is asking questions about narrative discourse that may or may not have something directly to do with the world-orientation of those fictions.[45] But the answers to those questions will help determine values of the world-oriented variables, since the number of characters will, among other things, affect the narrative density of the text and its character-system; the relations between them will shape its connectedness; how they are treated while "offstage" will determine the world's completeness; and the relation between density and character-system will generate the spatial dimensions of the work's amplitude. This example is enough to suggest, I hope, the degrees of mutual determination and overlap among the variables laid out here, and their operation within a larger system of meanings and interpretive practices.

---

45 See Franco Moretti, "The Novel: History and Theory," *New Left Review* 52 (2008). For an elaborate and interesting response to Moretti's claims about Chinese fiction, see Ling Hong Lam and Dahlia Porter, "Hybrid Commodities, Gendered Aesthetics, and the Challenge of Cross-Cultural Comparison: A Response to Moretti's 'The Novel: History and Theory,'" *Literature Compass* 7/9 (2010): 900–911.

And so, finally, the literary work as a relation to worldedness, but also as a relation to the world. But thus far, in the history of the philosophy of the aesthetic, a real difficulty seeing worldedness as a feature of the work of art proper—as though the plain, literal domain of the world (the real world, the actual world) were too complex or too distant from the world-creating force of the work to be the subject of its address. As though the aesthetic were somehow outside the sphere of world-production that would imagine the world as humankind's largest possible totality; as though the impulse toward "world" as a concept were too strong, or too weak, to include within its scope the idea that the literature itself might be the source of the world-idea. Hence "world literature" that is not about the literature of the whole world; hence "world-systems" that do not include the planet, or any real meditation on the nature of the world-concept they so effectively deploy; hence a "world picture" whose relation to history is at best Manichean, at worst completely idealized.

The question is not, How do we replace the adjectival and partial "worlds" that attach themselves to the idea of literature and literary systems with a holistic, all-encompassing concept that would unite, finally, the textual world with the material one? But rather, How can we think simultaneously the importance of "world" as a concept and synonym for totality, while connecting it to the problem of the greatest possible totality, whose other names in English are "human existence," "the earth," and "the universe"? It cannot be, though the world-systems theorists think it is, that the difference between the whole and a part that constitutes a whole—*the* world and *a* world—is merely one of degree. One hundred percent is not some degree of 75 percent; it expresses a movement beyond margin or limit, and transforms itself, at the margin and limit, into something beyond mere accumulation. (What happens to water at 0 degrees Celsius does not exclusively involve a change in the quantity of its temperature: so Hegel.) The world, however conceived, is not merely an instance of worldedness; it is the ground and frame for the instantiation of itself as a concept. And this concept, in turn, belongs in an especially intense (and perhaps necessary) way to the wholeness of the work of art, which enacts it, rejects it, alters it, or makes it into an emblem—and whose enacting, rejecting, alteration, or making is itself a meditation and reflection on the status of totality and worldedness beyond the work of art.

To name variables that would allow us to categorize and describe aesthetic worlds opens up two possible future directions for research in the history of literature. First, it compensates for an existing lack in the critical vocabulary, namely the absence of thematic-formal categories that operate in spaces and scales other than those of close reading (with its focus on the micro-genres of the anecdote, the moment, the sentence, the phrase, or the trope), genre (whose focus on macro-level structures is limited to particular *types* of form governed by restrictions in spatial arrangement or habits in conceptual pattern), or medium (whose differentiation operates largely at the level of disciplines and materials: visual art, digital literature, the codex, drama, and so on). As a category of analysis, the "world" is simultaneously formal and thematic/historical: the concept of wholeness it develops in relation to its own being as work can be related to social totalities or to the historical life of the planet, the Earth, or the globe, not to mention to its diegetic content (whose manifest focus, in the convenient cases of utopian or science fiction, will be world-construction itself).[46]

---

46 Thomas Pavel approaches such an argument when he compares, in *Fictional Worlds*, the historical and social circumstances likely to produce certain dominant strategies regarding the problem of completeness: "Cultures and periods enjoying a stable world view will tend to seek minimal incompleteness ... periods of transition and conflict tend to maximize the incompleteness of fictional worlds, which supposedly mirror corresponding features outside fiction" (108–9). But such moments in *Fictional Worlds* are few, and largely incidental to the more formal direction of Pavel's argument.

The second direction is comparative. "World," as a description of totality, may be a universal concept, in the sense that no work of art recognizable as such could avoid constituting itself in relation to a theory of wholeness that would, minimally, allow it to be recognized as a work of art at all. Comparative histories of this universal as it has been experienced and expressed, as it has been managed, ignored, or otherwise engaged, would cut across the existing barriers that divide works from one another on the grounds of historical time, language, or geographic location. We have very few categories that operate in a similarly broad mode—poetry and drama, perhaps, narration and description, perhaps, elegy and ode, perhaps.[47] None of them combine theme and form in quite the way the world does. Hence the range of references in this book. Though the texts themselves are to some extent arbitrary—it could just as well have been Balzac and Bessie Head, the *Dream of the Red Chamber* and *Chanson de Roland*, Satyajit Ray and *World of Warcraft*, and so on—their range is not. It demonstrates, I hope, the broad comparative applicability of this kind of *cosmographical* analysis, especially, perhaps, as it permits us to move across the less-frequently crossed boundaries of high and low culture, and of aesthetic medium, in addition to the more conventional ones of nation, language, and time.

The value of these categories thus lies in the connections they make between existing habits of literary analysis and new comparative analyses of a wide variety of works and modes of the aesthetic. My goal here has been to propose, first, a series of heuristic strategies designed to name and describe observable differences in the

47 On the possibly Eurocentric derivation of even so basic a category as "description," see Earl Miner, *Comparative Poetics: An Intercultural Essay on Theories of Literature* (Princeton UP, 1990). That said, without the category of "description" we might not be able to see that what some folks do isn't exactly "description" in the usual terms, and thereby develop a better theory of what those folks do, and what we do. The goal is to make better categories, not to endlessly lament their inevitable historical and geographic biases.

nature of the diegesis-producing work of art, and, second, by bringing them together with a number of strategies developed by others, to argue that they all describe parts of a larger whole, what I have been calling the world of the work. To say so is to insist upon the importance of "world" as the ground for those categories, and to assert that world's arrangement of theme and form, along with its historical relation to the very idea of the work as a made whole, make it an especially productive ground for the development of new categories of analysis. It is also to open a larger question, that of the relevance (and reference) of the notion of "world" to the actual or real world, which would allow us to ask whether the history of the world (as a social concept with a privileged relationship to the planet) has had anything to do with the history of the world of the work of art.

How, once we can describe an aesthetic world in a relatively rigorous way, might we begin to think its place, and, more broadly, the place of the work of art, in the total social history of the world as a ground for human life and human activity? To begin to respond to such a question one would have to have a good theory of the "total social history of the world as a ground for human life and human activity," if not for all time, then at least for some smaller period of it. With such a theory loosely in hand it should become possible to develop a historically minimalist framework that will permit the production of the history of the work of art as a history of worldedness. To come up with that theory, to develop that framework, and to produce such a history: these are are the three tasks of part 2 of this book.

PART II

MODES OF MODERN LITERATURE

Chapter 6

The Planet and the World

On a spherical surface, to leave one point is already to begin *to draw closer to it!* The sphere is Monotony.... This is where tourism began! From the moment man realized the world was a sphere.

Victor Segalen

World is a ground, but it is always the ground of *something*. This something is inseparable from the world as world, and relates to it as content to form. If history affects the history of world (as concept), then the something that the world grounds can also change the world as such.

Do changes in understandings of the nature of the world (as a place) affect the philosophical concept of world that purports to describe it? Does the history of perception of the planet (or the cosmos) shape the world-idea?

The Segalen epigraph suggests as much.[1] Only with the revelation of the planet as a sphere does the traveler's setting out become a tragically empty return. The sphere is Monotony: it brings you literally back to Earth. So too for this section of the book (the return to Earth, not the Monotony!). Let us turn from narratology to history, and examine the effects of the planet's history on the history of cosmography, the world-creating practice that remains largely

---

1 *Essay on Exoticism: An Aesthetics of Diversity*, trans. Yaël Rachel Schlick (Duke UP, 2002), 43.

idealized in Heidegger. For this examination, modernity—the idea of modernity—makes an especially appealing frame, since the historical break it announces is rich, or purportedly so, in planet-altering events. In Europe and elsewhere, capitalism, humanism, the Scientific Revolution, the voyages of the age of imperialism and discovery, the Reformation, colonialism and the forced and unforced migrations of people that attended it, transformations in the speed of communication and in the integration of markets for goods, in the distribution, storage, and processing of information, and so on: all these offer tremendous material for a historiography oriented toward transformation and change operating at the boundaries of the world-concept. That each of the types of change listed above has at one point or another been presented as the uniquely heroic (or villainous) source for modernity suggests how broad and intertwined the series of transformations is, and how much is at stake politically and rhetorically in the identification of one regime of transformation (capitalism, science, religion) as the origin of the others.

The general trends and transformations listed above are punctuated, historically, by a number of significant events, two of which are most literally relevant to world-making. I speak, first, of the series of cosmological and geographical revolutions leading from Ptolemy through Copernicus (*On the Revolution of the Celestial Spheres*, 1543) to Galileo and Newton, and, second, of the circumnavigation of the planet and the European discovery of the Americas, hermetically figured by Magellan (who did not complete his voyage, which ended in 1522) and Christopher Columbus.

In subsequent imaginaries, the two events are readily conjoined.

Again Vasco de Gama sails forth,
Again the knowledge gain'd, the mariner's compass,
Lands found and nations born, thou born America,

For purpose vast, man's long probation fill'd,
Thou, rondure of the world, at last accomplish'd

So Walt Whitman's "Passage to India." The lines that follow immediately place the rondure in its cosmological context:

O, vast Rondure, swimming in space!
Cover'd all over with visible power and beauty,
Alternate light and day and the teeming spiritual darkness,
Unspeakable high processions of sun and moon and countless
stars above, [...]
Now, first, it seems, my thought begins to span thee.[2]

The orthographic shift, rondure to Rondure, transforms action into
a proper name: rounding the planet reveals the Earth as Rondure.
This in turn permits the poet to grasp the Earth itself as a mariner,
"swimming in space," lurching toward whatever new accomplish-
ments the poem has in store.

Much has been said of Whitman's presentation of the world's
encirclement as an accomplishment. Indeed the poem presents that
navigational and (since the poem was written to commemorate the
1869 opening of the Suez Canal) architectural triumph as a historical one, a transformative act of completion that opens the door to
the possibility of a total poetic apprehension of the world, a justification, as Whitman puts it in the lines that follow, of the world's existence by virtue of its completion and its availability for thought:

The whole earth, this cold, impassive, voiceless earth, shall be
completely Justified,

---

2 Walt Whitman, "Passage to India," in *The Complete Poems*, ed. Francis Murphy
(Penguin, 2005), 431. Further references in the text.

Trinitas divine shall be gloriously accomplish'd and compacted
by the true son of God, the poet,
(He shall indeed pass the straits and conquer the mountains,
He shall double the cape of Good Hope to some purpose,)
Nature and Man shall be disjoin'd and diffused no more,
The true son of God shall absolutely fuse them. (432)

This is at some level just the usual Whitmanian bluster. Nonetheless the sentiment belongs to a centuries-long European program,
poetic, scientific, and philosophical, to incorporate the new shape
of the planet into existing concepts of history, of human life, and of
geological development. As Djelal Kadir has remarked, the cyclical
(well, elliptical) rotation of the planets and the circumnavigation
of the globe paired in Whitman's lines appear conjoined as early
as 1620, where we read, in Francis Bacon's *Novum Organum*, that
"although they [the ancients] had knowledge of the antipodes ...
yet that mought be by demonstration, and not in fact; and if by
travel, it requireth the voyage but of half the earth. *But to circle the
earth, as the heavenly bodies do, was not done or enterprised till these
later times:* and therefore these times may justly bear in their word
... *plus ultra* in precedence of the ancient *non ultra*."[3] In the prov-
identially ordained combination of the long-promised Christian
future and a factual, historical one, humans circle the earth "as the
heavenly bodies do": everyone's a star. From a figure for the limit of
knowledge, the "nothing beyond" (*non ultra*) stamping the edges of
medieval maps, to a figure for extension and possibility, the modern
plus ultra, is borne the extension of the geographic into the temporal, the opening not only of space but of time to the realm of action
and transformation.

---

3 Cited in Djelal Kadir, *Columbus and the Ends of the Earth: Europe's Prophetic
Rhetoric as Conquering Ideology* (U of California P, 1992), 43, my emphasis.

The practical integration of this New World of space and time into existing geographic imaginaries happened, as Kadir shows, through the cartographic response to Amerigo Vespucci's accounts of his four voyages to the Americas, which boldly identified the new lands as a fourth continent unknown to the ancients. The transition from the Ptolemaic imaginary to the modern one happened in visual form when Martin Waldseemüller, canon of the Church of Saint-Dié, published in 1507 a globular world map with an accompanying text, the *Cosmographiae Introductio*, that followed Vespucci in identifying the Americas as a fourth continent, and first proposed that they be named after him, their putative discoverer. Because cosmographical language of the time was largely Ptolemaic, however, the *Cosmographiae* is forced to describe a decidedly un-Ptolemaic world in fairly Ptolemaic terms. It thus teeters between an old vision of the world and a new one. The emblem of that precarious balance was, in 1507, a small globe, available for sale together with the map and the *Cosmographiae*. The globe and the map differed in one substantive respect: "For us, therefore, it has been necessary, as Ptolemy himself suggests, to place more faith in the information gathered in our times [than in older information]. We have on our map therefore followed Ptolemy, added new lands and some other things, while on the globe, which we have made to accompany the map, we have followed the description of Amerigo."[4] This imperfectly matched, self-contradicting set of world-representations captures perfectly the philosophical and practical tremble of its historical moment.[5]

4 Martin Waldseemüller, *The Naming of America: Martin Waldseemüller's 1507 World Map and the* Cosmographiae Introductio, ed. and trans. John W. Hessler (D. Giles, 2008), 107. The text was a collaboration between Waldseemüller and Matthias Ringmann, and was accompanied by a translation of Vespucci's *Four Voyages* into Latin. For a discussion of the globe, see Hessler, "A New View of the World," in *The Naming of America*, 51. On the decision to feminize "Amerigo" (as "America"), see Kadir, *Columbus and the Ends of the Earth*, 59.

5 Likewise for the two maps that originally constituted part of the book: "One of the maps, described in Latin as *in plano* (flat), is Martin Waldseemüller's famous 1507 World

That the circumnavigation of the planet had philosophical effects as well is clear enough if we consider the ramifications of the discovery that the globe's surface was for all intents and purposes finite.[6] A number of conclusions follow, as Immanuel Kant noted in his 1795 essay on perpetual peace:

> Hospitality means the right of a stranger not to be treated with hostility when he arrives on someone else's territory. [...] The stranger [...] may only claim a *right of resort*, for all men are entitled to present themselves in the society of others by virtue of their right to a communal possession of the earth's surface. Since the earth is a globe, they cannot disperse over an infinite area, but must necessarily tolerate one another's company.[7]

"They cannot disperse over an infinite area": the phrase imagines another, infinite world, in which there would be no right to hospitality or free movement, since on such a surface you could always get anywhere from anywhere. Only on a finite surface must we "tolerate one another's company," at least temporarily, with all the philosophical implications such a toleration implies. Though we normally refer to rights of this type as "universal" or "human" ones, Kant's sentences

---

Map, and the other, called *in soliodo* (in the round), was a printed globe gore of his design that is thought to be the first of its kind" (Hessler, "A New View of the World," 39).

6 This finitude, a necessary corollary of circumnavigation, brings about the return of *non ultra*, though this latter was for a long time mediated by those blank spots on European maps that motivate so much of the violence of Joseph Conrad's *Heart of Darkness*, and by various science fictional speculations, like those that imagined that the Earth at its antipodes opened up into an entire interior surface, occupying just slightly less square footage than the exterior one. Jules Verne's *Journey to the Center of the Earth* (1864) belongs to that general imaginary. Earlier examples included the anonymous *Le Passage du pôle arctique au pôle antarctique par le Centre du monde* (1721) and Captain Adam Seaborn's *Symzonia: A Voyage of Discovery* (1818; attributed to John Cleves Symmes Jr.). For more examples of hollow-earth theories and fictions, see Peter Fitting, ed., *Subterranean Worlds: A Critical Anthology* (Wesleyan UP, 2004).

7 Immanuel Kant, "Perpetual Peace: A Philosophical Sketch," in *Kant: Political Writings,* ed. H. S. Reiss, trans. H. B. Nisbet (Cambridge UP, 1991), 105–6.

suggest that whatever concept of universality obtains in the notion of a right belongs, first and foremost, to the literal place of its justification: all rights are "world" rights, particular to the world they derive from and apply to. From such a perspective, world is the "first" of first philosophy, the home of philosophy. Every philosophy expresses, somewhere, a theory of the world that it is a philosophy of.

The European reactions to the circumnavigation of the world paralleled, and intersected with, the astronomical revolutions of Copernicus, Galileo, Newton, and others, which remade the universe just as radically as Magellan and the others had remade the planet. Together these revolutions altered normative understandings of the cosmos and of the nature of space inside it, replacing a "finite and hierarchical universe" with an "indefinite or even infinite" one, and substituting for the "the Aristotelian conception of space—a differentiated set of innerworldly places—that of Euclidean geometry—an essentially infinite and homogenous extension."[8] These changes thus rewrote the (imaginary) physical framework of human existence. A detailed history of their impact, written by Alexandre Koyré, shows early clashes between the knowledge of the ancients and the facts provided by observation and experience; the slow working out, through letters, debates,

8 Alexandre Koyré, *From the Closed World to the Infinite Universe* (Johns Hopkins UP, 1957), 2. Though it has become a sociological commonplace to describe the cumulative effects of this transformation as a tremendous loss of humankind's privileged position at the center of the creation, as Koyré notes, some late medieval writers took the possibility of infinity as anything but a disaster. For Giordano Bruno, burned at the stake in 1600 for refusing to recant his philosopho-theological proofs of the infinity of the universe, "it is with a burning enthusiasm—that of a prisoner who sees the walls of his jail crumble—that he announces the bursting of the spheres that separated us from the wide open spaces and inexhaustible treasures of the ever-changing, eternal and infinite universe" (43). (The astronomers were more careful, and more divided—Kepler for instance had good philosophical arguments for believing that the universe could *not* be infinite.) On Bruno, see Ingrid Rowland, *Giordano Bruno: Philosopher/Heretic* (FSG, 2008); and Djelal Kadir, "Memories of the Future: Giordano Bruno Remembers Us," in *Memos from a Besieged City* (Stanford UP, 2010), 83–107.

disputes, state violence, philosophy, and further research, of the physical, metaphysical, and quotidian implications of these new facts; and the gradual and total dominance, ideologically and normatively, of the new world-view. The unveiling of infinity, like elaboration of new continents, only slowly and with great intellectual and social difficulty worked its effects on everyday European life.

Among the most prominent of these effects, and one particularly relevant to the study of aesthetic worlds, is the condensation and compression of the realms of human activity effected by the change from the Ptolemaic to the Galilean universe. For the former, life on Earth belonged to one of several spheres of cosmological action. Its meaning was necessarily reflected and shaped by the activities of the other spheres, including the stars, planets, angels, the Greek and Roman gods, and the Christian one.[9] By the time of Leibniz's acrimonious exchange of letters with Newton's disciple Samuel Clarke in 1715–16, however, the universe was reduced to at best two spheres of relevant causal activity—that of God and that of everything else.[10] And though the sphere of "everything else" had been enlarged to infinity, the compensation of an infinite field

9 See, for instance, Bernadus Silvestris's *Cosmographia* (ca. 1147). Silvestris's epic articulation of the Ptolemaic cosmological order with the necessities of God-created humankind leaves no doubt as to the basic theoretical integration of the problem of humanity and the order of the universe. "The *Cosmographia* reflects nothing less than the attempt to create a new poetic world, taking the Platonic cosmology with its neo-Platonic accretions as a model, but at the same time keeping all of this continually in perspective, using it as a foil to the presentation of a larger view of reality," Winthrop Weatherbee writes in his introduction to the text (*The Cosmographia of Bernardus Silvestris*, trans. Weatherbee [Columbia UP, 1973], 59). The crucial phrases here are "a new poetic world" and "a larger view of reality," which (though the latter reveals Weatherbee's bias toward the modern version of "reality") indicate Silvestris's complex ambitions.

10 And even then, for Leibniz, two would be too many, since God, having established the best possible universe at the level of its laws and structures, could essentially not intervene actively in it. On Leibniz and Clarke, see Koyré, *From the Closed World to the Infinite Universe*, "The Work-Day God and the God of the Sabbath," 171–97; on Leibniz and the best of all possible worlds, see Stephen Nadler, *The Best of All Possible Worlds: A Story of Philosophers, God, and Evil* (FSG, 2008).

of play (undivided by ontological differences or membranes) did little to mitigate the practical effects of its discovery, since no one was going to get off the planet to manage it. Since the new infinite universe was understood to be made of essentially the same stuff as everything else, its expansion of the realm of human cosmological engagement in *spatial* terms amounted to a reduction of that engagement in allegorical and symbolic ones.[11]

What Koyré calls the "geometrization of space" thus radically altered the spatial ontologies of human action and worldly constraint. Recalling the variables developed in part 1, we may describe that geometrization as a transformation of the world's *metadiegetic structure* in which narrative relations organized around ideas of sequential, physical cause and effect supplanted the dominance of a set of largely allegorical relations between activities at different "levels" of the Ptolemaic cosmological sphere. The differentiation of a figural logic from a narrative, scientific one inherent in such a shift gives us, among other things, the current senses of "astronomy" and "astrology," terms that before the seventeenth century had been largely interchangeable. Experienced as a trauma and a loss, this change appears, also, in these famous lines of John Donne's:

And new Philosophy cals all in doubt,
The Element of fire is quite put out;

11 This is not to say that philosophy should not attempt to be responsible to the real physical possibilities opened up by the new universe. We see one instance of such an attempt when Jean-François Lyotard begins, in *The Inhuman*, to take account of the philosophical implications of the inevitable cooling of the Sun, and wonders what it would mean to be responsible to the idea that humanity must, to survive (in the very long run), leave the planet (*The Inhuman*, trans. Geoffrey Bennington and Rachel Bowlby [Stanford UP, 1992]; incidentally, in the process of becoming a black dwarf, the Sun will double its size, evaporate the oceans, and turn the Earth into a ball of molten lava, so perhaps no one will be left to witness its cooling in any case). That said, we cannot expect to argue, contra Kant, that there is no right to hospitality because the universe is infinite, since the mechanisms for taking advantage of that infinity do not (yet) exist.

The Sunne is lost, and th'earth, and no mans wit
Can well direct him where to looke for it [...]
'Tis all in pieces, all Cohaerence gone,
All just supply, and all Relation.

That terrifying Relationality was explicitly linked, in Donne's cosmographical *Anatomy of the World* (1611), with the new technologies of global description, mapping, and navigation:

For of Meridians, and Parallels
Man hath weaued out a net, and this net throwne
Vpon the Heauens, and now they are all his owne.[12]

Relationality's geometrizing effects thus extended, literally and metaphorically, to such paired concepts as the sacred and profane, and beyond them, as any number of scholars have noted, to ideas of public and private, valuable and invaluable, the circulating and the fixed, the noble or the villainous, and so on. At its far reaches it included, too, the forms of rationality governing the intellectualization of modern life, described by Max Weber: increasing intellectualization and rationalization mean "that principally there are no mysterious incalculable forces that come into play, but rather that one can, in principle, master all things by calculation. This means the world is disenchanted."[13] In a geometrized world, not just space,

12 John Donne, *The Complete English Poems* (Penguin, 1977), 276, original spelling retained. As Stephen Toulmin notes, the cosmological language in Donne's poem reflects a sense that his readers will be largely familiar with a world-view in which the cosmos reflects the actions of the human life-world: "in underlining the interconnectedness of psychological and political issues with those that are cosmological and physical, he represents them to us as *aspects of a single whole*" (*Cosmopolis: The Hidden Agenda of Modernity* [U of Chicago P, 1992], 67). But of course the modern world-view also saw a "single whole": we are dealing here with radically different theories of the nature of wholeness, not (as Donne thought) the difference between a whole and a bunch of disconnected parts.

13 Max Weber, "Science as a Vocation," in *From Max Weber: Essays in Sociology*, trans. and ed. H. H. Gerth and C. Wright Mills (Routledge, 1991), 139.

but *everything*, became describable, fungible, transactable, translatable, exchangeable, and, finally, knowable.

Between the sixteenth and eighteenth centuries the European view of the world thus underwent a series of transformations that reshaped the cosmologies of both everyday and historical life. The implications of these changes, and their extensions in a variety of fields, continue to govern us today.[14] The world Europeans discovered and affirmed, and the universe that surrounded and expanded it, were no simple reflections of burgeoning capitalism, the Protestant ethic, or the Treaty of Westphalia. Had they been, they would have been incorporated with far less dissent and difficulty into existing structures of power and knowledge. The cosmos discovered and invented, experienced and narrated in those years was never, we must recall, the one Columbus or Copernicus set out to discover—nothing about the universe they described, or the globe they encountered, could be described as the simple expression of a desire (or a power structure) that preceded description or discovery. This is so even if, after or during the fact, the cosmos's role in the modern *Weltanschauung* owed almost everything to the pressures placed upon it by capitalism, imperialism, technology, religious reform, and the like—even if, that is, the integration and incorporation of the modern cosmos into the social, philosophical, and political structures governing Europe meant that the new cosmological discoveries were effectively "interpreted" or translated into

---

14 It would be too simple to make the direct sources of these changes—the circumnavigation of the globe, the Copernican revolution—the sole causes of the other great upheavals that coincided with those centuries, allowing them to become the "base" or cause of modernity (and hence of capitalism, the modern nation-state, and so on). World-transforming events in astronomy and navigation participated in a total cultural complex (or shifting series of complexes) in which a number of factors, including the rising importance of experience to knowledge and the European desire to access valuable East and South Asian trade networks, played vital, overdetermining, and occasionally incommensurable roles.

forms that were felt to be roughly compatible with those structures' existing needs.

The world, or worlds, that come out of that long process of mutual influence and interference, of influence, interpretation, and unforeseen consequences, express, singly and multiply, the world-picture of modernity. They become the physical and philosophical ground for the ideas of human history and human possibility that govern contemporary debates on the nature of the universe, but also, and more important, for the basic sense of the ontological and physical structure of everyday life and the simplest questions about the relation between the universe and the human.[15] There is never a moment when this world-picture can be cleanly separated from the other major determining forces of modernity. Nor can we easily separate our explanations of those forces from their assumptions about and relations to the world-picture that grounds them, and gives shape to their possibilities, transformations, and desires.

15 For a review of contemporary cosmological theories of parallel and multiple universes, including a discussion of anthropic arguments for the existence of this universe, and all universes, see Michio Kaku, *Parallel Worlds: A Journey through Creation, Higher Dimensions, and the Future of the Cosmos* (Anchor, 2005). At that level of abstraction, contemporary cosmological debates differ little from the ones among Leibniz, Malebranche, and Spinoza of three centuries ago.

Chapter 7

Universalism as a World View

So: modernity. I assume it exists, and that it is characterized as the social condition and world view produced by a collocation of events and forces occurring from the sixteenth through the nineteenth century, which include capitalism, imperialism, religious reform, and the scientific, philosophical, and political revolutions, each of which has been intertwined with each of the others, and each of which spins out a series of sub-events and sub-forces (the printing press, enlightened monarchy, vaccinations) that cross-pollinate and interact in turn.[1] Whether there *is* a modernity outside of the rhetoric or discourse of modernity seems to me immaterial. What matters is that since the early nineteenth century (beginning with Hegel) "modernity" has named the period of the political, cultural, economic, and military dominance of the globe by this alleged social condition, which runs from roughly the seventeenth century to the present.[2]

Any explanation of what modernity is and why it occurred must attempt to answer the question of universal history with which Max Weber prefaces his collection of essays on the sociology of religion: "What chain of circumstances led to the appearance in the West, and only in the West, of cultural phenomena which—or so

---

1 For an even blander definition that, like mine, attempts to be maximally responsible to the general cultural consensus on the matter, see Anthony Giddens: "'modernity' refers to modes of social life or organisation which emerged in Europe from about the seventeenth century onwards and which subsequently became more or less worldwide in their influence" (*The Consequences of Modernity* [Stanford, 1990], 1).

2 Named it, and so explained it: in the most basic sense to name is to explain, to assert a self-consolidating difference from a norm, to elevate from the background of the world some feature whose coherence is always already an argument about the nature of the real.

at least we like to think—came to have *universal* significance and validity?"[3] Weber's most famous answer to that question appears in *The Protestant Ethic and the Spirit of Capitalism*, in whose 1920 edition Weber significantly added the prefix "modern" to the words *capitalism*, the *capitalist spirit*, and *capitalist enterprise*.[4] The change restricts the "*universal* significance and validity" of Western rationalism to a particular historical period, whose name it then sets alongside capitalism as a kind of historicizing modifier. Weber's addition of "modern" thus directs us to the appearance of the universal in history—the arrival of the universal as a history-making event—that lies at the core of the philosophy of modernity expressed a century earlier by Hegel. The name "modern" invokes more than capitalism, more than just a single process or dimension of the lifeworld; it constitutes rather an attempt to grasp the wholeness of the world as the function of the arrival of the universal in it. In subsequent arguments the appearance of "modernity" is therefore always a signal that the discussion has been dominated by a theory of historical periodization and by the self-composing logic of an "era" that grasps itself as a totality and a world in its own right. For this reason the various attempts to rescue the possibility of the universal located in modernity, by resolving the problem of the totalizing subject (as in Habermas), by returning to it an abandoned early modern humanism (as in Toulmin), or by imagining modernity's various successors (Giddens, Castells, Hardt and Negri), will reproduce the historicist categories of the modern, "tak[ing] us back to the paradoxes and aporia of 'modernity' at a higher conceptual level."[5] Modernity is,

3 Max Weber, "Prefatory Remarks to *Collected Essays in the Sociology of Religion*," in *The Protestant Ethic and the Spirit of Capitalism* (Penguin, 2002), 356. Jürgen Habermas begins with a similar citation from Weber in *The Philosophical Discourse of Modernity*, trans. Frederick G. Lawrence (MIT, 1987), 1.

4 Peter Baehr and Gordon C. Wells, "Addendum on the 1905 and 1920 Versions of *The Protestant Etnic*," in Weber, *The Protestant Ethic*, xxxvii.

5 Peter Osborne, *The Politics of Time: Modernity and Avant-Garde* (Verso, 1995), 20.

for these reasons, both despite and because of the conceptual difficulties it presents, the essential horizon of "universal" thought.[6]

That paradox need not detain us much, so long as we recognize that this self-reflexivity confirms the intensity of modernity's relationship to the universal, since only through an endless series of self-reflections can modernity include itself in the universal that it aims to describe (and which, being universal, must therefore include it). In this the philosophical structure of modernity resembles that of the universal as such.[7]

Because concepts of the universal, like concepts of the world, can be historicized, we can conclude that modernity is a theory of the world—of a particular world. It is also, therefore, a theory of worldedness, *of a particular kind of worldedness that it most commonly calls the "universal."* We have seen with Kant how the classically modern notion of a universal right to hospitality can derive from factual information about the planetary surface. My argument here is that that episode in Kant can be abstracted out to modernity at large, whose relation to its own universality must therefore be understood as, also, a relation to the world that it "discovers" and that it imagines as the ground for its appearance in human history. Modern universalism is, in other words, quite literally the modern world-view. It phenomenalizes, at the level of the world-concept,

6 This discussion leaves aside several important uses of "modernity," and its cognates "modern" and "modernization," in more popular political and cultural discourse. But here the analysis is simple, since the terms are most frequently used by actors interested in (A) recreating a singular model of world history and economic development modeled on the recent European trajectory, very much connected to the major international institutions of neoliberalism (the IMF, the World Bank, and so on), that justifies a great deal of state and economic violence; and (B) making invisible explanations of that violence (including Marxist ones) that would imagine any future other than a continuous expansion of the economic and political system that characterizes the wealthiest and most powerful countries in the world.

7 On the unusually particularist mindset of European universalism circa the early twentieth century, see Christopher Bush, *The Floating World: Japoniste Aesthetics and Global Modernity* (Columbia UP, forthcoming).

a historically specific experience of the world. Like all lived hege-
monies, modernity is essentially a *process* in which the implications
of that experience are put into play, contested, habituated, altered,
resisted, and distributed across the field of social life.[8]

What are the effects of this world-view and of this universalism
in the history of the application and spread of "modern" thinking
(thinking, that is, that is universalist in orientation) across the surface of the planet over the last several centuries? We have seen one of
them in the discussion of the "geometrization of space," which flat-
tens the preexisting Ptolemaic hierarchy into a non-ontologically
differentiated plane whose every extension and folding can be
described in a single language. Descartes: "the matter of the heav-
ens and of the earth is one and the same, and there cannot be a
plurality of worlds"—at least, Koyré explains, "if we take the term
'world' in its full sense, in which it was used by Greek and medi-
aeval traditions, as meaning a complete and self-centered whole."[9]
Descartes's "one and the same" world is "not an unconnected multiplicity of such wholes utterly separated from each other," but "a
unity" composed of "an infinite number of subordinate and interconnected systems."[10] *There cannot be a plurality of worlds*: in this
phrase of Descartes's lies the core of the entire modern world picture. All the violence and hope bound up in the modern project has
depended on it.[11]

---

8 On lived hegemony as process, see Raymond Williams, *Marxism and Literature*
(Oxford UP, 1977), 112.

9 Can I also say, in passing, what a fantastic parataxis is the "and" that follows
Descartes's comma.

10 Koyré, *From the Closed World to the Infinite Universe* (Johns Hopkins UP, 1957),
105; the Descartes is from *Principles of Philosophy*, in *The Philosophical Works of Descartes*,
trans. Elizabeth Haldane and G. R. T. Ross, vol. 1, 265.

11 Descartes's language, and indeed the more general language of seventeenth- and
eighteenth-century possible worlds debates, reappears frequently in later descriptions of
modernity. Hence Niklas Luhmann: "Under modern conditions ... only one social system
can exist. Its communicative network spreads over the globe.... It provides one world for
one system; and it integrates all world horizons as horizons of one communicative system.

That the stars, sky, and earth "cannot be many, but only one," as Descartes also wrote, can be extended from the immediate realm of its application, physics, to a number of other areas of modern life and thought. This extension allows us to see in it a major general principle of modern universalism: a general collapse of levels that assures the absolute transactability and exchange of all forms of biological, physical, social, historical, and cultural life. Nature "is always the same and everywhere one," Spinoza wrote (in 1677, thirty-three years after Descartes). "Her virtue is the same, and her power of acting; that is to say, her laws and rules, according to which all things are and are changed from form to form, are everywhere and always the same; so that there must also be one and the same method of understanding the nature of all things whatsoever, that is to say, by the universal laws and rules of nature."[12] That this sentence appears in Spinoza's *Ethics*, at the beginning of a section called "On the Origin and Nature of the Emotions," suggests how broadly the seventeenth century's drive toward single-worldedness reached. It achieves one limit in what Spinoza called the "common notions" that constitute the ground and goal of reason, which govern not only the emotions but indeed all aspects of everyday life, where they form, Gilles Deleuze notes, "a mathematics of the real or the concrete," a quasi-biological "natural geometry that allows us to comprehend

The phenomenological and the structural meanings [of 'world'] converge. A plurality of possible worlds has become impossible" ("World Society as Social System," in *Essays on Self-Reference* [Columbia UP, 1990], 178).

12 Throughout natural philosophy (which included physics), the idea that "nature is always the same," Ken Robinson writes, was "fundamental to the new Weltanschauung" of the seventeenth century ("The Book of Nature," in *Into Another Mould: Change and Continuity in English Culture 1625–1700*, ed. T. G. S. Cain and Ken Robinson [Routledge, 1992], 84). Robinson also cites the Spinoza passage, which is from the first paragraph of part 3 of *The Ethics* (in *The Essential Spinoza: Ethics and Related Writings*, ed. Michael L. Morgan, trans. Samuel Shirley [Hackett, 2006], 61).

the unity of composition of all of Nature and the modes of variation of that unity."[13]

As with the Cartesian relation of a single world composed of "an infinite number of subordinate and interconnected systems" (Koyré), in Spinoza the understanding of the universal laws and rules of nature immediately reached out to include the "modes of variation of that unity" (Deleuze). We must recognize this seemingly paradoxical combination of universalism and multiplicity as central to the entire modern world-view. Its amalgamation of parts into a universal whole is in almost every case guaranteed by locating that wholeness somewhere at the bottom of an ever-increasing number of parts, as either their atomistic and material first principle, or as their systemic and legal one. Recognizing this double movement allows us to put modernity's universalism together with its equally powerful tendency toward differentiation, in which the rupture of a "global and mythic (but more often religious) overall dynamic" produces a variety of subfields with "distinct laws and dynamics."[14] The distinctions between economics and politics, the market and the state, the law and the courts, the home and the church, or the aesthetic and the useful belong to this general regime of differentiation and separation. There too one finds the fracturing of a singular normative world-view into multiple perspectives, what conservatives

13 Gilles Deleuze, *Spinoza: Practical Philosophy*, trans. Robert Hurley (City Lights, 1988), 56–57.

14 Fredric Jameson, *A Singular Modernity: Essay on the Ontology of the Present* (Verso, 2002), 90. This tendency toward multiplicity, differentiation, and fracturing acquires, in certain explanations of modernity, a purely formal quality. The most powerful example of this tendency comes in the systems theory of Niklas Luhmann and others, whose strengths in describing the modernity's past do not extend, as Jameson complains, to an ability to imagine anything like an alternative future. In his analysis Jameson explicitly connects Luhmann to Descartes, reading the latter's decision "to divide each of the difficulties I wanted to examine into the smallest possible units necessary for their better resolution" as "the foundation of empiricism as opposed to dialectical thought" that will lead to the informatic certainties of systems theory (86). What Jameson calls "differentiation" in his analysis of Luhmann resembles what I am calling, via Koyré, geometrization.

call "cultural relativism," in which the "reflexivity that developed in the modern program not only focused on the possibility of different interpretations of core transcendental visions and basic ontological conceptions [... but] gave rise to an awareness of the possibility of multiple visions that could, in fact, be contested."[15]

The seeming contradiction between these two poles, universalism and differentiation, is resolved by the relocation of the universal impulse to a different, more atomistic level. The separation between economics and politics as distinct fields of human activity (with their own distinct and apparently autonomous institutions, and so on) does not create two "worlds" but two "systems," as Descartes might have it, governed in the final instance by the same set of laws and belonging to the same logics of institutional development, evidentiary procedure, and so on (these latter the ideal *forms* of modern thought, not simply members of a neutral explanatory toolkit). Likewise, it is the atom (or the quark, in any case the idea of the smallest particle) that all matter has in common. That some atoms end up in houses and others in people (or expressed as energy) is essentially a matter of local concern, just as, for strict forms of structuralism or systems theory, differences among social institutions or myths belong to a set of formal systemic patterns whose logic, though it plays itself out in historical time, has little to with history in any of the usual senses of that word.

Today, the most self-reflexive grasp on this combination of infinite differentiability (on one hand) and a constant formal unit or law (on the other) appears in the actor-network theory of Bruno Latour, where distinctions between material and immaterial objects—or semiotic, physical, and social forces—have diminished so as to maximize, in every analytic situation, our sense of their constant interactions and interpenetrations. At this level any

15 S. N. Eisenstadt, "Multiple Modernities," *Daedalus* 129.1 (Winter 2001): 4.

of the usual ontological differences between things (or people and things) are revealed to be socially constructed. Social analysis proceeds by observing the gradual breakdown of old social patterns into conformity with this model, or by claiming that the social patterns have had the structure of an actor-network all along.[16] The major effect of this heuristic approach to social life is to produce ever-more-geometrized analyses of the everyday, for which the argument that the contemporary world places a new "premium on *activity* [for the sheer sake of activity], without any clear distinction between personal and even leisure activity and professional activity," made by Luc Boltanski and Ève Chiapello in *The New Spirit of Capitalism*, may serve as an illustrative example.[17] Here we see how the method of actor-network theory merges with what it illuminates; its logic belongs first and foremost, like that of all the best heuristics, to the system and world that it describes, and which it therefore formalizes and replicates.

As the example of the collapse of "personal and even leisure activity and professional activity" suggests, the geometrization

16 Bruno Latour, *Reassembling the Social: An Introduction to Actor-Network-Theory* (Oxford UP, 2007).

17 Luc Boltanski and Ève Chiapello, *The New Spirit of Capitalism*, trans. Gregory Elliott (Verso, 2005), 155. Consider in this context Jonathan Crary's analysis of the goals articulated by Eric Schmidt, the CEO of Google, for the next century's information economy: "The goal here is the continuous interface, not literally seamless, but a relatively unbroken engagement with illuminated screens of diverse kinds that ceaselessly solicit interest or response.... [O]bviously Eric Schmidt's model at Google is the unrelenting collapsing of any separation between the personal and professional, between entertainment and information, all overridden by a generalized and compulsory functionality of communication that is inherently and inescapably 24/7" (Crary, "On the Ends of Sleep: Shadows in the Glare of a 24/7 World," delivered at the Museu d'Art Contemporani de Barcelona in 2006, full text online at http://www.macba.cat/uploads/20070625/QP_08_Crary.pdf). Whether this tendency toward collapse belongs to a "third spirit of capitalism" that abandons the Fordist model in favor of networks, as Boltanski and Chiapello argue (or Crary seems to believe), or whether it represents the continuation of a more general process of geometrization that did not begin, or end, with Fordism (and will not probably end with networks), is beyond my scope here, though my money is on the latter.

of Nature first enacted in the cosmological sphere extends to any number of fields of human life. These include the rise of combinatoric (and digital) logic in the fields of military science, music, social organization, information storage, aesthetic production, the stock market, and, of course, human labor. Anthony Giddens refers to the products of this rise as "symbolic tokens," "media of interchange that can be passed around without regard to the specific characteristics of individuals or groups that handle them."[18] Among the most important of these is money, which abstracted and made potentially equivalent a wide variety of objects and behaviors, including labor and time, that had not been universally reducible (in quite the same way) in earlier periods.[19] As Peter Osborne has argued, the homogenization of labor-time produced by capitalism (via money, and the clock) led to "a generalized social imposition of a single standard of time," which in turn allowed for the "synchronization of actions," including historical actions, "on a planetary scale." For

18 Giddens, *The Consequences of Modernity*, 22.

19 Here Giddens channels Marx: "Money is the absolutely alienable commodity, because it is all other commodities divested of their shape, the product of their universal alienation. It reads all prices backwards, and thus as it were mirrors itself in the bodies of all other commodities, which provide the material through which it can come into being as a commodity. At the same time the prices, those wooing glances cast at money by commodities, define the limit of its convertibility, namely its own quantity. Since every commodity disappears when it becomes money it is impossible to tell from the money itself how it got into the hands of its possessor, or what article has been changed into it. *Non olet* [it does not stink], from whatever source it may come" (Karl Marx, *Capital*, vol. 1, trans. Ben Fowkes [Penguin, 1992], 205; see also Marx's discussion of Aristotle and value on 150–52). These remarks (which appeared in 1867) on the geometrizing function of money may be compared to the famous dictum of the *Communist Manifesto* (1848), taken up by Marshall Berman as a figure for modernity, "all that is solid melts into air," by noting the slightly differing attitudes they have to the transformation of what one might call the metasocial and metaphilosophical structure of premodern life (Berman, *All That Is Solid Melts into Air* [Penguin, 1988]). The sentence that begins "all that is solid melts into air" ends by claiming that in the modern world "man is at last compelled to face with sober senses, his real conditions of life, and his relations with his kind" (Karl Marx, *The Communist Manifesto* [Oxford UP, 2008], 6). The path of transformation is thus not from premodern "solidity" to modern "air," then, but from solidity to the "real conditions" of life—the previously solid melts into air, yes, but the resulting social field is far from vaporous or evanescent, as Berman notes.

Osborne, "capitalism has 'universalized' history, in the sense that it has established systematic relations of social interdependence on a planetary scale ..., thereby producing a single global space of temporal co-existence or coevalness, within which actions are quantifiable chronologically in terms of a single standard of measurement: world standard-time."[20] The effects of this general imposition of a single standard of historical time, which philosophically have their origins in Hegel, continue to structure the West's role as a geopolitical category "through which the historical predicate of modernity is translated into a geographical one, and vice versa."[21] This "capacity to *construct* a single historical context for everything is," Dipesh Chakrabarty writes, "the enabling condition of the modern historical consciousness."[22]

The breakdown of fixed forms into ever smaller, ever more recomposable units (in the movements of Taylorized factory work, for example[23]) has as its ground a theory as universalist in its atomism as any speculation of Descartes on the nature of other worlds. Once the general theory is in place it too can self-reflexively turn into a feature of a more general, quasi-formalist universalism—so that the common language of human labor in Taylorism and the common language of information storage in digital media become,

20 Osborne, *The Politics of Time*, 34. The relation between historical coevalness and the history of the European social sciences has been extensively theorized by Johannes Fabian, who notes that "allochronism is expressive of a vast, entrenched political *cosmology*," in *Time and the Other: How Anthropology Makes Its Object* (Columbia UP, 1983), 159.

21 Ibid., 16.

22 Dipesh Chakrabarty, *Provincializing Europe: Postcolonial Thought and Historical Difference* (Princeton UP, 2007), 243 (my emphasis). That this arrangement of space and time differed from the medieval, cosmo*graphical* one, we may gather from Gargantua's advice to his son Pantagruel: "Let there be no history which you do not hold ready in memory: to help you, you have the cosmographies of those who have written on the subject" (François Rabelais, *Gargantua and Pantagruel*, trans. M. A. Screech [Penguin, 2006], 48). This is the model of the potential utility of history as a feature of a general world-view, whose application in the present would operate, then, only allegorically.

23 See Martha Banta, *Taylored Lives: Narrative Productions in the Age of Taylor, Veblen, and Ford* (U of Chicago, 1995).

in effect, metonymies for each other, aspects of a more general atomistic and geometrizing logic governing the concept of modernity.
Hence Jacques Attali, in a book on the philosophy of noise, moving
in the space of two sentences from the history of classical music
to the history of the factory production and work: "Once each
function is decomposable into a polynomial, each noise becomes
decomposable into elemental sounds and recomposable into large-
scale aggregates of instruments. Capitalism was to translate this
proposition into: 'all production is decomposable into a succession
of simple operations and recomposable into large-scale factories';
efficiency required, for a time, gigantism and the scientific division
of labor."[24] The principle of (de)composition, like the principle of
digitization that follows it in the imagination of contemporary
history, is simply another variant of modern rationalization, sym-
bolization, and geometrization. To find its logic in music, as Attali
does, is immediately to connect music to the atomized logic of
modernity in general (here the factory, but it could have been anything). The form of resemblance that makes music not merely *like*
the factory but an expression of the *same logic* as the factory's is a
likeness that modern thought endlessly rediscovers. Together they
belong to what Ernest Gellner has called a "universal conceptual
currency" in which "all facts are located within a single continuous
logical space, so that statements reporting them can be conjoined
and generally related to each other, and so that in principle one
single language describes the world and is internally unitary; or
on the negative side, that there are no special, privileged, insulated
facts or realms, protected from contamination or contradiction by
others, and living in insulated independent spaces of their own."
Not for nothing is that passage cited in Franco Moretti's analysis

24 Jacques Attali, *Noise: The Political Economy of Music* (U of Minnesota, 1985), 65.

of descriptive practice in the work (and modernity) of Sir Walter Scott.[25]

The mutability of this form of likeness, its own universalizing and differentiating principles, so applicable to such a broad variety of forms of social practice—money and capital, signs, signifiers, and symbols (in short, information), concepts of the body or of affect, or forms of social, civil, and historical time—should keep us from tying it too directly to the circumnavigation of the globe or the cosmological revolutions. The literal is not necessarily the origin of the metaphorical. Nonetheless the general malleability and applicability of geometrization, which allows it not only to describe the geometrized world, but to enact through that description the geometrizing habit it observes, illustrates the degree to which modernity's universalism is, well, universal. Geometric universalism (which is to say, the particularly *modern* version of universalism) is a basic feature of the modern world-view. It is also an unconscious ground of modern social institutions, epistemological structures, and daily experience—including the experience of the natural world as such.

The "global" is the latest iteration of this world-view. And though this means that the global is, like the modern world-view itself, "an instituted perspective that brings objects into view and makes them available for and as truth," one that has "an interventionary or productive force," as Sanjay Krishnan has argued, this does not alter the fact that the global is also "a comprehension of the world as a single bounded and interconnected entity developing in common time and space."[26] It is precisely in this role as a "comprehension of the world" that the idea of the "global" acquires the power Krishnan ascribes to it. Though one can, to be sure, describe the global as a

---

25 Ernest Gellner, *Nations and Nationalism* (Cornell, 1983), 21; Franco Moretti, *Atlas of the European Novel, 1800–1900* (Verso, 1998), 45.

26 Sanjay Krishnan, "Reading Globalization from the Margin: The Case of Abdullah Munshi," *Representations* 99 (Summer 2007): 40–41.

historically particular version of the modern world-view, one non-identical in some respects to the view held by, say, Spinoza's small circle of Amsterdam friends, we also do well to recognize that for all intents and purposes the global, like so many of modernity's cognates and spinoffs (modernization among them), serves largely to elaborate a single vision of historical development. This vision makes the European model circa 1500–2010 the universal measure of all human culture and human history—and thus reinforces the basic presumptions of two hundred years of scholarship on modernity, from Hegel, to Weber, to Giddens, and beyond.[27]

The modern world-view, the feeling of modernity, is perhaps most simply the feeling that one lives in the same world as everyone else, that the rules governing history, physics, economy, communication, culture, space, and time, are the same everywhere and for all time: a general geometrization of the various measures of the universe. The period we call modernity sees the dramatic rise to prominence of this world-view, and its imposition via culture, economy, and violence on people with other views. To refer to "modernity" as a cultural formation, then, is to refer to a particular kind of perception of the world. One may say that an era or a society or a person is "modern" if each holds or is governed by this perspective (in general—we should not expect too much consistency).[28] Modernity is by definition exclusive of other possibilities.

* * *

27 Stuart Hall: "the global is the self-representation of the dominant particular" ("Old and New Identities, Old and New Ethnicities," in *Culture, Globalization, and the World System: Contemporary Conditions for the Representation of Identity*, ed. Anthony King [U of Minnesota P, 1997], 67).

28 In practice, modernity's universalism, the arrangement of measure and law that renders all entities transactable, exchangeable, or intercommunicative, does not happen all at once. Historically, modernity, like all culture, spreads differentially, unevenly, through violence, love, apathy, or desire. The world at any given moment is never fully modern, even if it is full of people whose basic world-views are.

These claims about the modern world-view will lead, in the next section, to a series of propositions about the kinds of attitude aesthetic objects can take toward that view, and thence to a more general theory of modern literature as such. Before moving on, however, it seems important to address the arguments, often taken up to resist modernity's Eurocentrism, that there are or have been "multiple" modernities. Such arguments see, correctly, that modernity's rhetorical and social force, its dominance of the philosophies of our present and our future, come from its alleged singularity, its "universal significance and validity," as Weber had it. They aim to diminish that force by either (A) locating within the temporal period of modernity other forms of modernity that offer alternatives to the Euro-American model of development and culture (transatlantic modernity, Confucian modernity, and so on); or (B) making European modernity one of a larger pantheon of moments of historical modernity (Susan Stanford Friedman suggests the Mongol world or medieval Timbuktu) characterized by many of the same social and economic features that have been described as the causes or origins of European modernity.

I am sympathetic to the general goal of such arguments to diminish the Eurocentrism of our historical narratives and to open up the possibility for transformations in the current world-system (by positing, for instance, a "trans-modernity" held in reserve in the corners of the planet least touched by Europe).[29] Nonetheless, the claim that Europe's modernity is just the latest iteration of a general type of cultural transformation (involving urbanization, technological

---

29 Enrique Dussel, "World-System and 'Trans'-Modernity," *Nepantla: Views from the South* 3.2 (2002). It may well be that, as Jameson argues, "radical alternatives, systemic transformations, cannot be theorized or even imagined within the conceptual field governed by the word 'modern'" (*A Singular Modernity*, 215). Proposals to rethink the nature of modern temporality (as, for instance, via the "everyday"), explored extensively in Osborne's *The Politics of Time*, represent an attempt to describe and make possible, inside the modern, those places where its general logic does not seem to reach.

change, clashes between cultures, increased levels of literacy, and so on), must contend with the historical realities of degree and kind. I do not doubt that there have been other such transformations, any more than I doubt that the history of this particular transformation, down to the appearance of its name, modernity, is an effect of Europe's political, philosophical, and cultural interest in imagining itself as historically unique. We must still recognize that, like philosophy, history is always the history of this world and this planet. As far as our particular modernity is concerned, that means noting the force of its newly conceived and discovered (conceived *as* discovered) relation to the planet and the world, and recognizing that no other modernity-like transformation before it had ever been able to locate its world-view so firmly in the specific spatial extension of the globe and of the cosmos, which constitute, after all, a new type of limit for the cosmographical imagination. That imagination and that limit coincide with the general theorization of modernity as universal, both conceptually (the whole planet = the universal, the view of the planet as, in, and from space, etc.) and materially (the connection between "discovery" and imperialism, circumnavigation, trade, and capital, settler colonialism, American silver, and so on).

That uniqueness produces the historical consciousness of the modern world-view. You do not encounter the planet this way twice.[30]

---

30 The claim that there are multiple modernities is perfectly compatible with a modern one-worldist model as imagined by Descartes: a single world, composed of multiple sub-systems, each of which is finally governed by the same laws (which are the laws of systems and sub-systems). To conceive those various sub-systems in the general dialectic of the moment, so as to activate the potential for transformation of the present, is, however, a deeply modern ambition. So probably one modernity after all.

Chapter 8

Realism, Romanticism, Modernism

Among other things the analysis above suggests that modernity may be an especially fertile ground for the analysis of aesthetic worlds, since the conjunction of literally world-shaping and world-shattering events produces a concomitantly heightened awareness of worlds, worldedness, world history, world literature, the globe, globalization, and so on. Though it may well be that other periods or places have dominant, culture-creating world ideas (Heidegger suggests as much), world's importance to modern thought, especially historical thought, means that it has exerted an especially strong conceptual pressure on the production of literature (and indeed art in general). What follows lays out a theory of modern literary history as a series of linked responses to the modern world-view.

Imagine, then, that we could call any work basically oriented toward the modern world-view a "modern" work. To be oriented toward a world-view (or by it) does not necessarily mean agreeing with it. "Modern" works would not therefore necessarily replicate the world-view, acting as vehicles for the representation of the geometrization of space, time, and so on. But they would *respond* to that view; they would position themselves in relation to it, interact with it in some way. At a bare minimum they would take its status and stature for granted.

In this respect modernity's best avatars in the media have been, as Benedict Anderson famously observed, the newspaper and the novel, which present their readers with a "'homogeneous, empty time,' in which simultaneity is, as it were, transverse, cross-time, marked not by prefiguring and fulfillment, but by temporal coincidence, and measured by clock and calendar."[1] One can appreciate some of the force of this world-view for the work of art by seeing in Anderson's description of the activity of the daily newspaper—occasionally, remember, called *Le Monde* or *The Globe*—a powerful expression of representational "completeness": "if Mali disappears from the pages of *The New York Times* after two days of famine reportage, for months on end, readers do not for a moment imagine that Mali has disappeared or that famine has wiped out all its citizens. The novelistic format of the newspaper assures them that somewhere out there the 'character' Mali moves along quietly, awaiting its next reappearance in the plot."[2]

This reification of simultaneity, which Anderson places at the heart of the national project, also describes the general universalism of the modern world-view. The relation to representational completeness encoded in social forms like the novel or the newspaper conceptualizes that universalism, and codifies and explains it.

1 Benedict Anderson, *Imagined Communities: Reflections on the Origin and Spread of Nationalism*, rev. ed. (Verso, 2006), 24–25.

2 Ibid., 33. That Anderson's example involves a famine is no real accident, since one of the potential forms of geometrization carried forward by modernity belongs to the realm of moral philosophy, where the relationship between the local and the global finds its most puzzling and controversial dilemmas around the issue of *care*. Adam Smith, wondering why a European might be more upset about a lost finger of his own than about the deaths of thousands in an earthquake in China; Immanuel Kant, noting that now "a violation of right in one part of the world is felt all over it"; Peter Singer's suggestion that we develop "the ethical foundations of the coming era of a single world community": all these respond to the imperative to think through the forms of justification and recognition that individuals and states owe to others, and to consider the strong importance proximity plays as a determinant in the distribution of care or the recognition of the other as having rights. Kant, *Perpetual Peace: A Philosophic Essay*, trans. M. Campbell Smith (London, 1917), 142; Singer, *One World: The Ethics of Globalization*, 2nd ed. (Yale UP, 2004), 198. On the geographic limits of sympathy, see Eric Hayot, *The Hypothetical Mandarin: Sympathy, Modernity, and Chinese Pain* (Oxford UP, 2009).

But of course not all novels reify simultaneity the same way. In fact, one can think of novels in which the easy reifications of time encoded by the newspaper are called into question, undermined, or simply ignored (one common narrative apparatus for this gesture in twentieth-century fiction is repressed personal or historical memory, whose trauma prevents time from ever moving forward, producing something like a vertical rather than a horizontal simultaneity of time—consider something like Dambudzo Marechera's *Black Sunlight*, or Freud's case studies). We can also think of works that organize time in ways that fracture the notion of simultaneity itself, in which the entire organizing logic of events frustrates the transactability of universal time, producing multiple forms of temporality that resist cumulative reconciliation (Kurosawa's *Rashomon* is perhaps too classic an example).

Is it possible to develop a typology of these various responses to the proposition of a world-view? Could such a typology be used to redescribe the literary history of the modern period, and, if so, what would that history look like?

Let's find out. As with the categories developed in part 1, which here will come into some use, my goals are not systematic but heuristic: to design concepts that will allow us to see new things in works we already know, to imagine new types of family resemblance across works, and to disrupt, beneficially, existing models of comparison and similarity by opening them up to novel forms of difference. The following thus proceeds by laying out a minimalist set of *logical* responses to a proposition. Far from designating the concrete reactions that govern any specific and historical human community, as Jameson once said of the semiotic structures of A. J. Greimas, the logical qualities of the responses aim to describe the empty slots and possibilities that necessarily obtain in relation to all propositions, and hence to all human communities in which propositions are made.[3] Below, the responses are generally described in relation to the general modern world-view that I have outlined so far. But as I suggest both here and in the appendices, the derivation of those historical specificities from the modern ought not to suggest either that the modern is the only field of their possible applicability, or that it has any especially inventive or original relation to them.

AFFIRMATION AND CONCEPTUALIZATION: REALISM

From one of the earliest fictional apprehensions of the modern world-view—I am speaking here of Miguel de Cervantes's *Don Quijote*—the world-organizing, world-creating impulse of the novel has taken as one of its subjects its own self-production as a world. This not only because the contrast between *Don Quijote*'s eponymous, zany jouster and its hoi polloi shows us identical phenomenological inputs producing radically different interpretations (windmill or giant, inn or castle?), but also because the ten-year gap between the novel's two volumes saw the publication of a competing second volume of the Quijote story, Alonso Fernández de Avellaneda's "false" *Quijote* of 1614. A year later, in Cervantes's second volume, many of the minor characters have read both prequels, and the encounters between Sancho, his don, and these strangers offer our heroes an occasion to rectify the "lies" of the Avellaneda version, as Sancho does in a conversation with Don Gerónimo: "The Sancho and the Don Quijote in that book have got to be different people from the ones in [the Cervantes book], because the ones in *his* book are us: my master is brave, and wise, and madly

---

3 This sentence rewrites and cites a sentence from Jameson's *The Political Unconscious: Narrative as a Socially Symbolic Act* (Cornell UP, 1981), 46.

in love, and I'm just a plain fellow with a good sense of humor, and no glutton and no drunkard."[4] In the possibility of contestation about the truth of a fictional character, in an intertextual dialogue's casual violation of the boundary between work and world, we see the modern artwork probing the edges of its own ontological status.

Don Quijote is a text about the refusal of its main character to agree to the cosmological premises universally adopted by the novel's minor characters, or even by extradiegetic author-narrators, who the novel treats as so many other contestants in the game of accurate representation. Quijote's refusal is tragic for him, comic for the rest of the novel, and it is as a comedy plot that we must read the triumph of the world occupied and created by the combined power of belief of the novel's panoply of minor characters (and indeed by the narrator, who knows, after all, that *Don Quijote* is not sane— that part of the book the hidalgo has not read well). This belief creates the substrate against which Don Quijote's imaginary world is measured, found inadequate, and made into the stuff of narrative. The shared world the characters of the *Quijote* live in is, because it is shared and naturalized, the world of the modern.[5]

Don Quijote thus thematizes a self-conscious modern "yes," an affirmation of the ontologies of the modern present that nonetheless recognizes the imposition of that present as the product of a necessary struggle, in which insanity takes on the normalizing role that Foucault had identified for it in *Madness and Civilization*. The novel's "yes" is counterposed to Quijote's "no," a no that despite its rejection of the world everyone else lives in does not constitute a

---

4 Miguel de Cervantes, *Don Quijote*, trans. Burton Raffel, ed. Diana de Armas Wilson (Norton, 1999), 674.

5 The novel gives us a world that can be seen in two ways; it is also a document that exemplifies the possibilities of seeing the actual world in two ways. On the relationship between exemplification and world-making, see Nelson Goodman (from whom I have borrowed the delightful phrase "zany jouster" in the paragraph above), *Ways of Worldmaking* (Hackett, 1978), 104n10.

refusal of the general ontology of the modern. For the don's conscious insistence is not that there are two worlds, but that there is one, and that it is his. The novel's challenge to single-worldedness resides in the difference between the collective's yes and Quijote's no. As readers of the second volume know, *Don Quijote* ultimately sides with its minor characters, leaving the Mancha's hidalgo nothing for his efforts but a cascade of regrets and a mouthful of broken teeth. This closure, which is merely the violent dental synecdoche of the physical and emotional beatings the don suffers over the course of seven hundred pages, shows us the modern period producing "that very life world, that very 'referent'—the newly quantifiable space of extension and market equivalence, the new rhythms of measurable time, the new secular and 'disenchanted' object world of the commodity system, with its post-traditional daily life and its bewilderingly empirical, 'meaningless,' and contingent *Umwelt*—of which [the novel] will claim to be the [...] reflection."[6]

Nonetheless the novel as a whole opens up a realm of self-conscious thematization of the modern world-view that begins with Quijote's emphatic refusal of social norms. This latter has its formal counterparts in the novel's character-system and metadiegetic structure. In the former, as we have observed, the distribution of world-views among major and minor characters results in a novel in which protagonism, major-ness, consists primarily of the refusal of a dominant world-view, without which the hero would have no reason to act. (This may be one fate of the epic hero in modern narrative: brought down to earth, located in the same world as everyone else, the hero distinguishes himself [as Raskolnikov seems to] by daring to belong to another world entirely.) As for the metadiegesis: it is Quijote's insistence on the identity of the allegorical and the diegetic-realistic, his demand that (what others call) allegory

6 Jameson, *The Political Unconscious*, 153.

dominate and shape the world of the minor characters, that causes his adventures to begin. The string of failures that stubborn demand produces in the diegetic sphere is compensated for, at novel's end, by Quijote's recuperation as a symbol. This is how we end up with the tragic notion of the quixotic: it is the symbolic retrieval of the fantasy of two-worldedness from the realm of the diegetic. The "lesson" of the novel is thus a lesson, also, about the arrangement of the symbolic, the allegorical, and the diegetic in modern storytelling.

All of this is to say that *Don Quijote* presents, thematically and formally, a series of cosmological arguments that amount to a strong case for the aesthetic mode that I will here call Realism.[7] Realism is empirical and world affirming: it is "not merely a set of stylistic and narrative conventions, but a fundamental attitude toward the relationship between the actual world and the truth of literary texts," as Thomas Pavel has written of its lowercase cousin.[8] It frames, conceptualizes, and normalizes the cultural experience of a period. In modernity, therefore, it establishes imagined communities, teaches people how to think about the world as the product of shared spatial and temporal logics, and reinforces the sense that any narrative takes place against the backdrop of an ongoing historical and geographic structure that functions—as the world does, in the modern imagination—relatively independently of the activity of any given story.

Described this way, Realism sounds ideologically normative. And at some level it is, though how so exactly depends on how the Realism of any given text appears as theme and form. There are many ways to say "yes," including the quiet and largely unmentioned reproductions of the modern world-view in the vast majority

7 Having named this mode, whose differences from a lowercase-r realism I will describe in a moment, I can retroactively reinsert the word *realistic* to the citation from Jameson of two paragraphs ago, where I had replaced it with ellipses.

8 Thomas Pavel, *Fictional Worlds* (Harvard UP, 1986), 46.

of fiction, or in newspapers, where the ideology of the modern mar-rows the bones, sustaining itself there against all Quijotes past or present. Whereas, in stark contrast to such indolent affirmations, in Cervantes we see one-worldism challenged, disrupted, and trium-phant, in any number of modern works of art the geometrization of social and physical life and the affirmation of the "normal" world-view is earned far more cheaply, so cheaply in many cases that it costs nothing at all, and is never discussed in the text. Such works do not mention Realism; they use it. Together they constitute the majority of acts of world-making (in any era).[9]

What is the relation between Realism as a mode of world-orientedness and "realism," the term used to describe certain features in the development of the aesthetic during the modern period? Realism (the mode) distinguishes itself from realism (the historical practice) insofar as realism, as I am using it here, names the dominantly normative representational strategy *particular to the modern period*, while Realism as a mode names the dominantly normative representational strategy of any period. In this latter, more structural sense Realism, unlike realism, is not the product of a particular historical consciousness—it is a possibility inherent in a system of meaning organized around a world-view, one which in some other period or social sphere might not be realist at all. As a mode, then, Realism, unlike realism, is not discovered. No one gets progressively "better" at it, leading finally to a representational acme (in, say, certain British or French novels, in photography),

9 The radical world-orientation of Cervantes's novel is reflected, perhaps, in the ini-tial impulses of the novel's printers, who sent the majority of the first print run to the "new" world. Though most copies were lost in a shipwreck, some seventy copies made it to Lima (see Serge Gruzinski, "Une mondialisation venue d'Espagne," in *L'Histoire* 322 [August 2007]: 30). In 1607, two years after the novel's publication, "a small mining town in the highlands of Peru awarded its first prize, during a festive ring joust, to impersonations of Don Quijote and Sancho" (Diana de Armas Wilson, editor's introduction to Cervantes, *Don Quijote*, viii–ix).

which in turn delivers a crisis (modernism, naturally). The latter sense of realism dominates many histories of fiction, including Bakhtin's essay on the *Bildungsroman* and Ian Watt's *The Rise of the Novel*, each of which describes a gradual progression toward a more-perfect capture of reality—as though reality itself remained stable over time, and humans simply improved their ability to represent it.[10] The historical logic governing such narratives is loaded with the language of invention and discovery, centered (as it often is in painting) around the use of a language of "technique" that simply replicates a classically modern progressivism that coincides, unfortunately, with the most Eurocentric of historicisms.

By imagining Realism as a mode, rather than as a practice, and by conceiving it as part of a structure of relation, I intend to dislocate its practice from (A) a static model of reality that assumes that the reality we moderns believe in has in fact been the only reality humans have ever had (rather than being itself a historical function); (B) from a model of progressive increase in representational capacity appropriate to that static and single reality that treats Realism as a discovered technique (or combination of techniques); and (C) from a theory of realism that grounds its aesthetic meaning and historical value purely in the circumstances of its historical

---

10 For Bakhtin, see in particular the history of the novel's gradual capture of the "real world" (Mikhail Bakhtin, "The *Bildungsroman* and Its Significance in the History of Realism: Toward a Historical Typology of the Novel," in *Speech Genres and Other Late Essays*, trans. Vern W. McGee, ed. Caryl Emerson and Michael Holquist (U of Texas P, 1986), 43–45 passim): though the description of the history of literary worldedness is compelling, phrases like "the process by which the real world was rounded out, filled in, and integrated reached its culmination in the eighteenth century" make his developmentalism perfectly clear (44). As for Watt, the notion of progression lies beneath his general treatment of the novel as a genre. Only the novel, through the development of certain techniques that respond to actual transformations in the world, "captures" reality. Other genres (the picaresque, e.g.) do not capture reality; they merely reflect it (they can thus be read as indexes of a world-view, but they themselves cannot show the world as such). The arrival of the novel is thus the arrival of the first storytelling genre to grasp reality as such (rather than to act out, in its failure to capture, the ideologies of its social form).

appearance in Europe, rather than seeing it as part of a system of representational modes whose appearance in a particular historical form is only one aspect of its overall historical significance.

The decision to name the mode Realism will entail some confusion, which I have tried to remedy by capitalizing the mode and leaving the historical practice in lowercase. To be clear: for the modern period, the normative mode Realism intersects significantly with the historical practice of aesthetic "realism"; likewise, as you will see, the Romantic mode (the mode of creativity and destruction) resembles and overlaps with "romanticism," and the Modernist mode (the mode of negation or refusal) corresponds in some respects to "modernism." My sense is that these essentially *partial* overlaps make the function of the modes, their basic character in the modern period, clearer than any alternatives, which mostly felt clunky and neologistic. The problem is thus not with the words *realism, romanticism,* and *modernism* themselves, but with the fact that they have been used to describe a literary historical narrative whose basic presumptions about the nature of history seem to me to be wrong. Hence my decision to retain and modify them, and by *détournement* to note both their proximity to, and dislocation of, existing literary historical narratives. Hence also the risks of such a decision, that the terms will, by virtue of their (true!) proximity to their cousins, once again reify a European progressivism in the realm of aesthetic history that it is my intention to undermine. (On the plus side, they may, by virtue of that same proximity, help with the undermining.)

CREATION AND DESTRUCTION: ROMANTICISM

The force of Realism at any given moment lies in its reproduction of the formal properties that govern the normative view that it reflects and responds to. Accordingly we may deduce, in reverse, the general world-view governing the middle of the twentieth century from a book like Erich Auerbach's *Mimesis*, whose strong sense of what realism does is governed by an equally strong sense of the "earthly" or "human" reality that realism represents. With some effort it would be possible to describe that apprehension at any given moment— perhaps by looking at all its artwork, or some representative sample thereof—by describing its relation to the variables developed in part 1 of this book.

There is, for instance, a "normal" and expected level of amplitude in the modern work of art, one whose violation in any respect will signal immediately that we are in the presence of an alternative world-imaginary. Likewise we can expect a "normal" level (and typology) of dynamism, of connectedness, or metadiegetic structure—levels or types we only know as "normal" by comparing them to the normal levels and types of works in different periods or different genres (the normal dynamic structure of the detective novel, in which history functions almost entirely as an inactive background, is quite unlike the normal dynamic structure of the highbrow nineteenth-century French novel, and so on). Forms of normalcy free the work for other things. Unless actually thematized, they operate as background or skeleton for content, or for types of form that are not themselves particularly world-oriented.

The Romantic mode shares with the Realist one the basic presumption of world-oriented normalcy. But where Realism is world-affirming, Romanticism is world-creating. In it the particular limits of the modern's empirical reality—its "content," from one perspective—are tested, reshaped, and reimagined. The "no" Romanticism speaks to a dominant world-picture does not reject the basic ontological or physical premises of its norm. Instead it alters the dominant's content, and that alteration highlights or causes to appear the parameters of its presence. (Think of Quijote, modern after all, insisting not on his right to see the world as he wished, but insisting, especially in the first volume, that the world he saw was the only one in existence.) The Romantic mode in the modern period imagines the world—one world—otherwise. Hence Jameson, speaking of the genre in history: "romance is precisely that form in which the *worldness* of *world* reveals or manifests itself, in which, in other words, *world* in the technical sense of the transcendental horizon of experience becomes visible in an inner-worldly sense."[11] By altering the affirmative premises of the world-representational norm, the Romantic mode makes appear the fact of the world, that is, the fact of its phenomenological and ideological force as world-view.

In the modern period Romance is thus the mode of utopias, and of science fictions, and of the cult of nature, which articulates its critique of modernity's technological substrate by proposing real or mental communions with a world untrammeled by technique.[12] By virtue of its appeal to a difference from the norm, the Romantic mode is heavily auratic, in Benjamin's sense; by illuminating the world's limitations, it envisions its uniqueness, and thus the possibility of its transformation, alteration, or loss. By not taking the world for granted, Romance restores to world the idea of its being a work; and if the world is a work, then it has been (and can be) made. Romantic works thus make visible the world's *contingency*. That is why Romance is the mode of the political and the politically

---

11 Jameson, *The Political Unconscious*, 112. Jameson's remarks on romance in *The Political Unconscious* draw on and extend those made in "Magical Narratives: Romance as Genre," *New Literary History* 7.1 (1975), where a near-twin to the first half of the sentence I cite above is followed by the remark that "romance as a literary form is that event in which *world* in the technical sense of the transcendental horizon of my experience becomes precisely visible as something like an innerworldly object in its own right, taking on the shape of *world* in the popular sense of nature, landscape, and so forth" (142). Part of my argument in this book is that the "technical" sense of *world* never escapes (and never just leads *to*, but also always draws [and draws away] *from*) the "popular" sense; there is (I repeat) no world-form without world-content, and vice versa.

12 On the valley as a utopian chronotope, for instance, see Darko Suvin, *Metamporphoses of Science Fiction* (Yale UP, 1979).

possible. (And why, historically, it is so strongly connected in the modern context to the European discovery of the New World. The narrator of More's *Utopia* [1516] was, after all, allegedly a sailor on Vespucci's 1504 voyages.)

From a material-formal perspective, we can observe that the creation of modern Romantic worlds, especially in the genres of fantasy and science fiction, will have a strong tendency to rely on the arrangement of fictions in series. The sense of completeness provided by the gap between novels assures the extension of the imaginary world beyond the boundaries of the fiction (just as does, *mirabile dictu*, the second volume of the *Quijote*). There—in the star treks and star wars, or in Balzac's human comedy—the worldness of the world (its modernity, in this case) is affirmed as much by the spaces between novels as it is by the novels themselves. The fictional series assures us of the singular modernity of its world-formation by imagining the persistence of time outside of the modality of its narratorial attention. (When Descartes wonders, in the *Meditations*, whether the world to which he wakes is the same one in which he fell asleep, he finds himself on the incipience of the modern.[13])

The intense relation between Romance and completeness suggests that the differences between Romance and Realism may simply involve a shift in the emphasis of certain formal features, rather than a wholesale disappearance of one or the other mode. This in turn implies that there is never in the art work such a thing as a pure Realism or a pure Romance. Any work arranges modes, balances competing interests, and aggregates formal and thematic choices. Together these may amount to a description of a work or an oeuvre, allowing us to translate the language of Lukács's essay on narration and description, into new terms: where for Lukács Balzac's Realism

13 Rene Descartes, *Meditations on First Philosophy*, trans. Donald A. Cress, 3rd ed. (Hackett, 1993), 14–15, 17.

makes the world visible in a new way (it is, therefore, in some important way Romantic), Zola's Realism simply affirms everything it sees (and thus does not create; it verifies but does not change anything).[14] In another realm of the aesthetic entirely we can observe that same set of tensions playing itself out in the history of photorealistic painting, where a Realism so extreme as to become Romantic undermines the premises of the normative world-view from, as it were, its insides.

No pure Realism: the modes are inter-implicated. We might begin to think about the relations among them as at least partly unequal. The Romantic mode, for instance, seems in the modern period heavily dependent—asymmetrically so—on the Realist one, requiring a bare accommodation of Realist norms in order to make its Romanticism legible. Can we imagine a society in which the reverse were true—in which it was the Romantic mode, the call to fiction, making and imagination, to make believe, that functioned as the asymmetrically vital ground of Realist work, and whose force needed to be reaffirmed quasi-ritualistically prior to any elaboration (Sing, O Muse!) of the worlding-event?

NEGATION AND REFUSAL: MODERNISM

The Modernist mode is world-denying: "down with all hypotheses that have allowed the belief in a true world."[15] Modernism (in modernity) represents situations—no longer worlds—in which no single shared experience dominates, in which communication becomes cacophony. This is why the literary-historical category

14 Georg Lukács, "Narrate or Describe?" in *Writer and Critic and Other Essays*, trans. Arthur D. Kahn (Grosset & Dunlap, 1971).

15 Friedrich Nietzsche, cited by Jean Baudrillard, *Simulations* (Semiotext(e), 1983), 115.

known as "modernism" is so frequently defined as a crisis in representation. But a crisis in representation is not the fundamental problem of modernist literature; the crisis is the effect or the ground of an attack on the basic cultural structure of modernity, on the very possibility of the geometrizing world-view that has come to dominate the planet over the past four hundred years.

A truly pure Modernist work would have to assert a total ontological rejection of the normative world-view of its era. To do its job perfectly well, it would have to be incomprehensible, not even recognizable as a work of art. In the modern period, some moments in Beckett, some abstract art, some concrete or sound poetry, some found (or declared) art, approaches this limit (but does not reach it). For the most part, accordingly, the Modernist refusal is leavened by doses of the Realist and the Romantic modes. Many of the writers we now call "modernist"—the Europeans and U.S. expats of the 1900–1940 period—largely combined Modernism and Romance, building new worlds from an apprehension of the diversity of world-experiences (think of *The Cantos*), while the stay-home U.S. writers of that same period tended, for reasons that would be worth exploring, to produce more Realistic work. We do the field of literature a disservice when we exclusively group these authors under one aesthetic rubric—as we almost always must do, given that our rubrics are so historically bound—or when we solve the problem of inclusion and difference by adducing to the rubric a clarifying adjective (American, Irish, rural, late), as though the "modernism" stayed the same the whole time. Among other things, I am suggesting that the study of literary history would be quite different if we were to regroup and recategorize the authors we have under a different explanatory logic, or even if we just had *more than one* explanatory logic at hand. More on this in part 3.

That a pure Modernism would be unrecognizable does not make it unique, but suggests that neither of the other modes described here can ever appear purely on its own, either. A purely Realist work would not be recognizable as a work, since its affirmation of the world would be so total as to cause it to merge seamlessly with the norm it reproduced. On any "made" thing, in the labor of creation and fiction, we discover the fingerprints of Romance. But pure Romance, likewise, would be inaccessible without an aperture into a viable and mutually recognizable Real, a way to get from here to there, be it a ship, a time machine, or a state of mind.

If no modality can appear in the art work entirely untouched by the others, literary history becomes a question of tracing shifts in the arrangement of modal forms, and in the distribution of those modalities in the work of art. The goal would not be to determine, however, how a work that is 33 percent Realist, 40 percent Romantic, and 27 percent Modern compares to one with the percentages reversed, but minimally to seek to redescribe some of the existing historical formations in other terms, and to use those redescriptions to create new kinds of comparative analysis. For instance, one may observe, in the transition from the modernist to the postmodernist work of art (using these terms in their conventional literary historical sense) something like a rebalancing of modes. More specifically, we might from a rough sense of certain key works assert that one important strain of British modernism (Pound, Eliot, Woolf, despite their differences) balanced a view of the world as heavily fractured, disparate, incomprehensible, and potentially irreconcilable (a Modernist view) with an equally hopeful imaginary of transformation, reconciliation, and change (a Romantic one).[16] This is the vision of modernism, too, in Jameson's famous reading of Van Gogh's peasant shoes, in which the appearance of the object opens up a whole world

---

16 That someone like Wyndham Lewis shares none of this latter measure of hopefulness (unless one reads misanthropy as a kind of disappointed idealism) suggests once again why it might be useful to have another set of categories by which to measure representational differences at the level of the world-view.

of labor and life, and the tension and greatness of the painting lies in the contrast between the shoes' silent modesty and the immense picture of the world they guarantee. If we take Jameson's privileged counterexample, Warhol's *Diamond Dust Shoes*, as the representative work of a certain postmodernism, we might begin by saying that in the latter the presence of the Romantic, world-creating mode has been almost entirely erased. The Modernism is still there—the representation of an object that barely belongs to a shared world, that threatens the dissolution of communication between viewer and image. But in Warhol the Modernism is, in a sense, Realist in mode: it takes as the world-*affirming* norm the fact of meaninglessness and noncommunication that the Van Gogh had worked to overcome. The combination of despair and hope that makes the Van Gogh what it is becomes in Warhol an acceptance, if not a celebration, of the Realism of Modernism as such: we live in a world in which objects do not communicate, and in which their silence (or their cacophony in another, inaccessible language) cannot and should not be redeemed or repaired by the aesthetic. American postmodernism's evacuation of the Romantic spirit that had governed so much of the work we now call "modernist" represents a return to Realism, a return that retains the Modernism of the earlier period, but tunes it to a completely new frequency.

Because this redescription of (a certain) postmodernism does not imagine that the world-oriented strategies the latter adopts belong solely to their historically unique expression in the United States of the 1960s, it makes possible a number of transhistorical comparative questions. One might ask, for instance, if similar shifts have occurred elsewhere—if, that is, any other time or place has seen an erasure or dissipation of the energy of a partially Romantic world-view and its replacement by a partially Realist one. This question is good for the past, but also for the future, since the nature of the "postmodern" turn now becomes an aspect of the historical elaboration of structure, one that is repeatable (with differences) in other situations later on. A general comparative analysis of such shifts, only one of which would have been known as "the postmodern," might describe the truth of a social form in ways that would give less immediate weight to the history of the American mid-century, even if it also recognized, as it should, that the particular history of that place and those decades had something to do with the appearance of the postmodern as we have known it. (Beyond modernity, if one defines "Realism" as the dominant world-view of any given moment, there would be norm-reinforcing Realisms of, say, ancient Rome, which might be inflected by Romantic or Modernist modes, and whose structure might be comparable to the American postmodern as well. More on this in the appendixes.)

One of the advantages of thinking of these modalities as structural expressions of a set of possibilities encoded in any given dominant system is, therefore, that it allows us to resist thinking their appearances in history as purely developmental (first Realism, then Romanticism, then Modernism). The modes are, instead, encoded in advance by the logic of minimal response to any social argument, even if their expressions appear to us in historical time. To misrecognize the ontology of events as purely developmental or successive, and to interpret their logic within the frame of innovation and origin, is to assume the most basic historical presumptions of modernity. Structural thinking lays bare, at least momentarily, such assumptions. In this alternative schema the appearance of a given relation to worldedness in a particular context might still emerge from local history, but the structural fact of its emergence would not in and of itself be historical. Or rather, it would be historical in the sense that the structural possibility would belong not to the history of British literature or the late eighteenth century but rather to the concept of modernity as a whole.

Chapter 9

Six Variables, Three Modes

Six variables, three modes. How are they connected?

The modes are not, first of all, purely collocations of particular combinations or degrees of the variables. To be Realist is not just to adopt a certain degree of amplitude, a particular kind of metadiegetic structure, a fixed measure of completeness, and so on. A mode is larger than its variables, because the mode becomes what it is at any given moment through the interaction between variables, the other modes, social norms, and histories of content and theme. Modes sum up a variety of parts.

If we ask, however, what effects shifts in normative world-ideas have had on arrangements of aesthetic world-space as expressed in the modes, we can measure some of those effects by looking at the variables, using the latter as proxies or figures for various aspects of representational change. Observe, for instance, the striking difference in the geometrization of narrative levels of Chaucer's *Canterbury Tales* (written 1369–72) and Boccaccio's *Decameron* (written 1350–53). In Boccaccio few if any moments in the telling of a tale change relationships among the storytellers. The distance between the framing metadiegesis and the story-based diegesis is held relatively steady, with very little "leakage" between them. The stories the characters tell reflect but do not significantly alter the storytelling space. In Chaucer, by contrast, the levels between (metadiegetic) narrators and (diegetic) narration are crossed by the effects of one telling upon the next, allowing the sphere of narration to resonate to the vibrations of the tales' events and morals. The tales become proxies for relationships among tellers, the relations between narrative levels producing, in effect, two plot structures that constitute an interlinked totality—two systems, but one world, as Descartes might have had it. The *Tales* thus dramatize a geometrization of narration and narrated and a fluidity of narrative "levels."[1] If we wanted to move rapidly forward to produce a comparative history of the geometrization of narrative levels, we could observe that the flattening of narrating and narrated levels reaches one kind of limit in the first two volumes of Sterne's *Tristram Shandy*, whose diegesis flourishes so beautifully under the weight of its narration, and another in the exploits of twentieth-century metafiction (where it has, of course, a completely different social function).[2] Together these amount to a bare outline of a history, or system of possibilities, of narrative geometrization. But such a history alone could not explain the function of that geometrization in each case. Unless you simply decide to make the *Tales* a precocious vision of an anticipated modern Realism (in which case you would have to explain why this vision manages to grasp modern Realism's geometrization at the level of narrative, but not its effects on, say, dynamism), you must explain this geometrizing effect in Chaucer as partly a function of the norms of late fourteenth-century England (or of some larger or smaller era or system governing it). Variables only mean in relation to the modes, and other variables, alongside which they appear.

1 This dynamism extends, as Alex Woloch has noted, to the character-system and forms of social completeness that appear as early as the *Tales'* prologue, which introduces a number of characters who never tell stories: "In this way the prologue includes the excluded, describing persons who have no voice, creating a kind of shadow between prologue and tales: the shadow of social extensiveness itself" ("Minor Characters," in *The Novel*, vol. 2, "Forms and Themes," ed. Franco Moretti [Princeton UP, 2007], 309).

2 In metafiction the move toward total geometrization of levels of narration attacks the representational world-completeness of the Realist mode, even as it confirms on an entirely different plane the continuity between fiction and "real life," fiction and reading. This is a case of carrying the variable "too far," passing beyond the boundary of the Realist norm and into Modernism. Metafiction, in breaking the fourth wall of fiction, thematizes the collapse of the Romantic function of the artwork.

As for the other variables, it is again a question of using them to describe shifts and changes internal to the modes, or differences among them. When it comes to amplitude, for instance, contemporary Realism resembles the Bible far more than it does Homer, despite some significant counterexamples (including, as I noted earlier, the television sitcom, which is recursively Romantic, particularly in its orientation toward historical time). Completeness moves, along the track laid out by modern Realism, toward the subtleties of the reality effect; and dynamism, as Bakhtin suggests, increases steadily in both scope and variety over the course of the development toward the *Bildungsroman.*[3]

Toward the *Bildungsroman,* but not too much further. Though the premodern to modern transition produces increases in the intensity of certain of the variables as they apply to Realism, and shifts in the quality of others, it is not simply a case of modernity pushing variables to their conceptual limits. There cannot be anything like an infinite amplitude, a total dynamism, or an absolute completeness. Though a text can try for effects that approximate those absolutes, the extremity of its efforts will tend to violate the social norms that establish a bare horizon of Realist expectation (which is why such attempts belong in general to Modernism). It is the nature of Realism and Romanticism to stop short of purifying the variables, as it is the nature of norms to represent themselves in relation to unchosen extremes. Realism thus trends not toward *infinite* amplitude but toward a socially and ideologically normative one, not an *absolute* dynamism (which would after all be awfully hard to read) but one in

---

3 In this sense dynamism seems highly related to connectedness and completeness, since the extension of immediate narrative effects both inward (toward psychology) and outward (toward politics or society) showcases an increasing sense of the existence of connections and a desire to insist on the locatedness of the instance of narrative inside a broader social field that includes it but does not require it.

line with the social beliefs of a given moment's, or fiction's, sense of historical possibility.

Similarly, it is not the case that increases in completeness in modern Realism get us closer and closer to the real world, until we finally arrive at ideal completeness and actual reality all at once. Realism develops, but not like a technology. To think of Realism as a technology is to mistake the historical development of European fiction in the eighteenth and nineteenth centuries—whose history we have tended to tell as a "progression" or series of improvements in the reality-capturing capacity of the representational during the modern period—for the logic of Realism as a whole.[4] The trajectory of world-oriented Realism is not toward an ever-increasingly accurate reproduction of reality but toward the *continuingly* accurate production, and reproduction, of the social and ideological norms of its world-picture. Speaking modally, the fundamental developmental force of the modern aesthetic is, generally, a highly Realistic Romanticism—since it is the latter that is charged, in the structure I have developed here, with the socially acceptable transformation of the Real. Insofar as the great historical realisms of nineteenth-century European fiction—Dickens, Stendhal, Dostoyevsky—produce a near-total or perfect version of what we think of today

---

4 I know, *pace* one of my best readers, that many literary critics do not narrate modern literary history as a continual and progressive improvement in the capacity of the artwork to capture reality. Nonetheless I insist that the generic discourse of the anthology, of the museum, or of the undergraduate course that covers the modern period has tended to reproduce that narrative, and has, in turn, narrated the achievement of a near-perfect realism (in the mid-to-late-nineteenth or early-twentieth century novel, or the Dutch still lifes) as both a triumph and a crisis in representation that leads into, or is loosely contracted to, modernism (still attempting realism) and beyond. Harry Levin, who does much to complicate this generic picture, nonetheless remarks (while ventriloquizing the same generic "we" that I do in the sentence to which this footnote is appended) that "[t]he novel, we say, has consistently moved in a realistic direction: in other words, closer and closer to reality, as continually reinterpreted with reference to a changing style of life and view of the world. This progression seems to be *normally irreversible*" (*The Gates of Horn: A Study of Five French Realists* [Oxford UP, 1966], 465). I have more to say about Levin and the general tendency he describes in chapter 14.

as reality, they do so by openly *imagining* that reality into being.[5] This is one reason why one might argue, as has Yogita Goyal, that we must account more completely for the persistence of romance in the novel form.[6]

This reference to the generally dominant mode of the modern permits a return to the larger historical picture that has been the subject of part 2, namely the premodern to modern shift. I have described the historical alterations in world-picture, what I have called the modern world-view, as producing a number of shifts in the nature of the modes, for which "geometrization" has served as a master figure. These shifts can also be parsed as variations in the values of the six variables, as follows:

- Significant increases in dynamism and completeness, especially through the nineteenth century, followed by shifts (but not necessarily increases) in the twentieth.

5 What I am calling Realistic Romanticism approaches what Donald Fanger called "romantic realism," in which "that the novelist does his best to record the real world is assumed; but his recording is *shaped by his vision of that world*, and his vision is inevitably a function of his autobiography—as personal and as inimitable" (*Dostoevsky and Romantic Realism: A Study of Dostoevsky in Relation to Balzac, Dickens, and Gogol* [Harvard UP, 1967], 15, my emphasis). Fanger differentiates between what he calls "pure" and "romantic" realism. From the modal perspective developed here all Realist works include at least some degree of Romance; no purity is possible. Nonetheless Fanger's claim that the romantic realists created "myths" that were organized around great cities is suggestive, insofar as it seems to point to the *world-creating* force of the Romantic mode, and to suggest that such a force was felt more strongly in certain authors than others. That's probably true *if we hold reality still*. But since the categories I develop here refer to normative, historical world-views, it may be possible instead to say instead that the difference between Balzac and Zola stems not from differing aesthetic responses to the same world, but from shifts in the dominant world-view *and* shifts in the aesthetic responses to it. (At the limit this kind of historicization, because one can always push "down" one level of specificity [from a century to a decade, a decade to a year, and so on], runs the risk of producing a "total" historicization of aesthetic production that is, unfortunately, completely incoherent, since it would have to argue that every work was simply a response to the conditions at the minute (or second) at which it was completed. Such are the limits of relativism.)

6 Yogita Goyal, remarks made during Q&A at the annual conference of the Society for Novel Studies, Durham, N.C., April 27, 2012.

- New levels of normative amplitude, especially in psycholog-ical and sociopolitical space, corresponding to new imagi-naries of the human character and of social life.

- A collapse of metadiegetic structure, generalizable as a shift from figuration to narration, and, within figuration, from allegory to symbol (hence a renewed interest in allegory in the Modernist mode, both in literary practice and aesthetic theory).

- In character-system, increased dynamism and variability reflecting (and codifying or reimagining) the geometriza-tion of socioeconomic space, as described by Alex Woloch.

- Alterations in the nature and structure of connectedness and networkedness, reflecting both the felt experience and transactional realities of globalization (the simple increase in awareness of long-distance connections, visible in the sympathetic revolution of the eighteenth century), but also an increased awareness of their importance and role in, for instance, social completeness (and hence a geometrization of social levels when it comes to the kinds of characters who are allowed to affect plot).

- Similarly, shifts in the nature of connectedness that manage the abandonment in the social sphere of concepts like fate or destiny, and their replacement by such imperfect modern corollaries as luck, circumstance, or coincidence (of which "small worlds" is but one instantiation).[7]

---

7 Dostoyevsky's *Crime and Punishment* registers this latter transition with remark-able sensitivity, emphasizing and meditating on it in a serious of unusual heterodiegetic and iterative prolepses in chapters 5 and 6 of part 1. There the narrator leaps forward to a Raskolnikov located outside the temporal frame of the novel, and ponders at length the relation between fate and coincidence (I have italicized words related to narrative time, and underlined those connected to fate): "When, *later*, he recalled this time and every-thing that happened in these few days ... he was *always struck* with superstitious awe by one circumstance, which, though not really very out of the ordinary, seemed to him after-wards to have determined his fate" (57–58); "But why, he *used to ask* himself, did such an

Insofar as these shifts and transformations reflect changes in techniques used for the reproduction of normative social and aesthetic space, they occur largely as events inside Realism. But of course shifts in the Realist norm lead immediately to changes in the nature of the Romantic and the Modernist modes, as well, since the taking up of a new structure, or the abandonment of an old one, frees that structure (or that arrangement of variables) for use in other modes.

The analysis of changes in the normative functions of the various world-variables can and must, therefore, be carried over to the level of the modes themselves. Changes in the arrangement of the modes—in the primacy of one or the other mode, in the development of schools or groups or trends that reconfigure their arrangements, as in the modernism-postmodernism shift—reproduces social form at another "level" of the aesthetic. Just as Realism models a normative sense of the modern world-view, so the relationship between Realism, Romanticism, and Modernism in the postmodern U.S. novel models a vision of that relation that is itself a higher-order statement about the world-view in the present.[8] Likewise one can describe naturalism as a movement in Realism that instantiates the Modernist, world-

important and <u>fateful</u> encounter for him take place.... It was almost as if <u>fate</u> had laid an ambush for him" (58); "And *in after years* he was *always* inclined to see <u>something strange and mysterious</u> in all the happenings of this time, as if <u>special coincidences</u> and influences were at work" (Fyodor Dostoyevsky, *Crime and Punishment*, trans. Jessie Coulson [Oxford UP, 2008], 60). I am grateful to Nathan Hensley, whose remark that "Henry James needed to account for probability," which he followed with the deceptively simple observation that you need events to have a plot, reminded me that managing coincidence becomes a significant narrative challenge for the secular, psychological novel precisely when it abandons the chronotopic patterns of the externalizing adventure plot (Hensley, remarks made during Q&A at the annual conference of the Society for Novel Studies, Durham, N.C., April 27, 2012).

8 We thus see that though we can make statements about the ways in which the premodern to modern shift has affected the variables or the modes *in general*, any particular example in action produces an arrangement that can both (A) be seen as a general example of some larger category to which it imperfectly belongs, or (B) be understood as the unique expression of its own particular set of choices. This is simply to reassert the importance of analytic scale as discussed in the preface.

negating mode by locating it in one of a series of privileged diegetic figures (the diseased woman, e.g.); modernism's relation to naturalism could then be described as at least partly as a function of the movement of that Modernist impulse from content (character) to form (language)—a movement that frees the modernist diegesis from the obligation of representing, among other things, poor people. Any given configuration of modes—which might be codified as a school, a movement, or the oeuvre of a single artist—ought thus to be analyzed both in relation to the general set of structural capacities that I have outlined here, and in relation to any number of potential historical and social contexts, from the small to the large. Any shift in the nature of aesthetic norms rearranges the total pattern of the variables and modes, which is why Pierre Menard's rewriting of the *Quijote*, in Borges, produces such a different text from the original.[9]

Together, then, the variables and the modes describe the history of a set of representational norms, and connect those norms to the social forces that they helped register and conceive. None of this means that the work of art always "discovers" society or the world, that it is invariably ahead of the imaginative curve whereby the social comes to be represented to (versions of) itself. We can only say that the artwork encodes and makes legible a set of relations that are expressions of a world-view in whose origin, conceptualization, development, consolidation, and transcendence works of art themselves play a vital role—and to which, through the commitment to making, the aesthetic will have a privileged and shared relationship. What emerges neither asserts art's reflective epiphenomenality nor illustrates its subordination to or illustration of history. It demonstrates art's coevality and engagement with the historical, and confirms its imaginative power and its verdant, social force.

9 Jorge Luis Borges, "Pierre Menard, Author of the *Quixote*," in *Collected Fictions*, trans. Andrew Hurley (Penguin, 1999).

PART III

IDEOLOGIES OF THE INSTITUTION

Chapter 10

Against Periodization

> If by some radical epistemic *boulversement*, we *were* able to drop periodizing altogether, that would in itself signal that we had left the modern behind—as long as it were not for still another period, for [...] that would be a sure sign that we were still thinking under the auspices of the modern.
>
> *Margreta de Grazia*

Spinoza: "every definition is a negation."[1] Negation is thus the life of thought: without it the totality cannot become parts; without parts there can be no relation.

The tendency of definitions to become second nature, however, means that they are also the enemy of clear thinking, its most habitual stopping-place. Though it is thus no news, and no crime, that definitions are negations in general, the particular forms of negation that organize our relations to one another and to the world merit continued, pessimistic vigilance.

Vigilance has, conveniently enough, some useful rules of thumb: strategies for managing and mitigating the partiality of our common negations. One involves authorizing, within a given field, a diversity of concepts or methods, in the hopes that the differences among

---

1 Spinoza, Letter 50 to Jelles, in *Letters*, trans. Samuel Shirley (Hackett, 1995), 260; the phrase *omnis determinatio est negatio* is translated by Shirley as "determination is negation," but is more often seen in the form I use above.

them will have a policing effect. Placed alongside other concepts, differently powerful and differently limited, a concept's limitations and powers spring into light. A field that includes scholars using both quantitative and qualitative approaches, or formalist and historicist ones, for instance, contains within itself an open (and sometimes hostile) dialogue on the viabilities of its major methodological choices. Within such a field the master concept governing any single work of scholarship (a particular idea of society, of the literary, of the performative) becomes a visible choice, which must be justified against unchosen alternatives. Congeries of concepts thus highlight a concept's perimeters, and rely on the awareness of differences *among* concepts to police the limitations of any single one of them.

A second major strategy for mitigating the partiality of concepts involves making room for the trans-conceptual or trans-methodological. In the humanities and social sciences, two major watchwords of that strategy—interdisciplinarity and transnationalism—adumbrate the primary limiting definitions of the study of human culture and human life, namely the disciplinary and the national, which constitute the major organizing principles of colleges of the humanities and the liberal arts. Such transconcepts disrupt the negations that constitute the core modes of institutional and intellectual life and, in so doing, belong intimately to the negations they disrupt. (The nation lies, after all, at the heart of the transnational, just as the prominence of disciplines gives interdisciplinarity its meaning and power. The transconcept is the bird cleaning the concept's mouth.) So conceived, transconcepts illustrate a given definition's immanent boundaries. They do not escape it; they constitute it as a system. By revealing the strictures imposed by the conceptual division of infinite space into units, they impose a marginal but sustained awareness of determination and negation within a given epistemological sphere. Together with the strategy of multiplicity (which highlights the external exclusions imposed by a given definition), the strategy of transconcepts (which highlights the internal ones) keeps scholars aware of the ways in which the evidentiary and definitional structures that make knowledge possible do so by making other forms of knowledge (or evidence) harder to see.

All this is obvious enough. But that obviousness makes it difficult to explain the near-total dominance of the concept of periodization in literary studies, a dominance that amounts to a collective failure of imagination and will on the part of the literary profession. We have failed, first, to institutionalize a reasonable range of competing concepts that would mitigate some of the obvious limitations of periodization as a method, and, second, to formalize in institutional ways transconceptual categories that would call our attentions to the boundaries periodization creates within the historical field of literature. Our collective desire to remain institutionally inside periods may be illustrated by the tendency to extend rather than cross periods—the long eighteenth century, now longer than ever; the early modern, reaching ever backward into the old medieval; or modernism, straining nearly entirely into the present—as a way of coping with the repeated recognition of the inadequacy of period, and its ostensibly permanent epochal boundaries, as a frame for the kinds of questions we wish to ask. The tendency to lengthen periods is stronger when the periods articulate concepts, which might lead us to believe that numerically neutral periods (not post–1865 U.S., then, but the raw name of a century) are somehow less conceptual than named ones. But all periods are concepts, even when they merely exclude other times, since the periodizing gesture only makes sense as a loose amalgamation of culture and historical similarity, a similarity reinforced every time someone says something like "the twentieth century"—about which we all agree, roughly, what it means.[2]

2 As long as we agree on the geographic region to which the phrase applies. "The twentieth century" means something awfully different in Europe than it does in, say, Latin America (and differently within those regions).

That we have failed to create alternatives to periodization can be confirmed by a simple look at the Modern Language Association (MLA) job list, which reveals, as it has every year for the past fifteen years and more, that the vast majority of job opportunities in literature, no matter the national field, are defined in periodizing terms. As the job list suggests, our failure expresses itself most clearly not in the heady conceptual arena, but in the *institutionalization* of the period as the fundamental mode of literary study at every level of the profession, from the job market to the undergraduate curriculum, the journals to the professional societies, the conferences to the comprehensive exams. And though we may be tempted to see the undergraduate curriculum as the root of this necessary evil, to do so requires forgetting that the faculty have made the curriculum. The curriculum is us. The system that it so visibly codifies is the same one that governs the training of graduate students and the production of dissertations, and on their basis the near-entirety of the early career labor of most professors in literature. No one should be surprised that, once tenured, those professors reproduce the norms under which they have thrived (or at least been trained) in a variety of institutional forms. Those forms precede them at every level of the institution.

In short, our entire system of literary education, from the first-year undergraduate survey to the forms of judgment governing publication, promotion, and tenure, reifies the period as its central historical concept.

Conceptual challenges to the currently institutionalized forms of periodization have been around since the early days of theory.[3] What is remarkable is that they have had so little institutional

---

3 As a reader of the manuscript pointed out, the title of the inaugural theory journal, *New Literary History* (founded 1969), signals an ambition to hold on to literary history while moving beyond existing historical models—a program replicated, to some extent, in this book.

effect, especially on the job market, where periodizing norms have become, in my experience, more rather than less prominent in the last decade or so. To some extent this reflects the ways that New Historicist approaches to literary criticism have become fully ideological and substructural, rather than being, as they were throughout the 1980s and early 1990s, subjects of intense critical debate. This victory of New Historicism is, like the victory of Theory itself, a tragic one: the measure of its triumph rests on the paradoxical disappearance of its force as a trajectory or a school, the loss of institutional memory and of the contexts of its initial emergence. Because almost everyone now thinks "new historically," no one is really a New Historicist anymore. The thinking is enough: it has inculcated a strong unstated theory of *era* as the final goal and subtending force of the intimacies of literary criticism, which reifies at an ideological level a powerful theory of periods as social wholes. This theory requires a vast expansion of the material necessary to master a single period, and produces, correspondingly, an increase in the force of institutional and intellectual barriers *between* periods, since crossing them now requires a level of understanding of the period as a self-contained whole that cannot be easily acquired: "the triumph of the specialist resulted in the much-remarked explosion of research in the subdisciplinary fields that made the old goal of coverage no longer tenable."[4] This in turn may explain the gradual foreshortening of the required historical "perspective" for PhDs in English: while twenty years ago the average new scholar of British literature could be expected to teach *Beowulf* to Woolf, and the U.S. scholar Columbus to *Goodbye, Columbus*, the kinds of historical

---

4 Jennifer Summit, "Literary History and the Curriculum: How, What, and Why," *Profession* (MLA, 2010), 145. On a related note, the relative loss in prominence *for literary studies* of the number of small, cultural-studies focused PhD programs built in the 1970s and 1980s—Stanford's Modern Thought & Literature, UC-Santa Cruz's History of Consciousness, Wisconsin-Milwaukee's Modern Studies—reflects the strong conceptual return to periodization.

knowledge now required to work inside periods make such long views increasingly difficult to achieve.[5]

None of this militates against the concept of the period in any specific way, or prevents one from recognizing all the great work done under its aegis (and under the rubric of New Historicism more specifically). It does, however, open the door to asking about the impact of periodization's dominance of scholarship in the humanities, which reflects badly on our collective awareness of the ideas governing our institutional and scholarly behavior. This failure of self-consciousness, the lack of debate over the value of the period as concept (especially now, after the acceptance of many postulates of literary theory), is what makes periodization ideological. Our response to the ideologization of periods ought to be to develop *and to seek to institutionalize* a variety of competing concepts, including trans-periodizing ones, for the study of literary history. This would ensure that the concepts themselves could become explicit (and contestable) subjects of scholarly work. The contests among them would then generate at a higher "level" trans-conceptual approaches, which would in turn prevent new concepts from easily producing new ideological calcifications.

We already have a few institutionally viable non-periodizing concepts. The MLA list includes every year a small number of jobs that do not make period fundamental. Some focus on genre (drama, novel, poetry, new media) or sub-genre (science fiction, children's literature), some define theoretical or social fields (the postcolonial, theory, women's studies, ethnic studies). These categories can of course be modified by period, but even when a scholar's research

---

5 This change is also, to be sure, an effect of decanonization, or recanonization, which has increased the sheer quantity of work for which one must be responsible in any given historical unit. The point is not to return to an earlier model of canonicity or periodization, but to carry the gains we have made over the last decades into new realms of literary historical institutionalization and thought.

focus operates within a relatively restricted historical field, the professional expectation requires an awareness of a far longer history and broader geography than most periods, especially later periods, require. Scholars of twentieth-century poetry must, generally speaking, know something about the ancient Greeks (if not yet the ancient Indians or Chinese), just as those who work on contemporary ethnic studies must have a sense of the historical development of their analytic categories, so that a scholar of black cultural expression in the 1990s United States, for instance, must possess a great deal of knowledge that extends back, transnationally, across several centuries: knowledge about the slave trades, the plantation economy, the Civil War, the migrations that followed it, and so forth.

To these existing non-periodizing alternatives we may add those recently proposed by Franco Moretti and Wai Chee Dimock, both of whom have directed scholarly attention to historicizable features of the aesthetic that are either smaller or larger than the particular work of art. For Moretti, these include such figures as free indirect discourse or the clue. Without straining we could expand this list to include the soliloquy, various aspects of narration, including forms of characterization or point of view, rhetorical microgenres (the joke, the anecdote), poetic features like rhyme, figures like apostrophe or hendiadys, or other newly described or invented features of rhetoric, narrative, or form. Dimock meanwhile has focused on a few far larger conceptual units (kinship, planetary time, the epic) that make visible, subtended by close reading, novel connections across the spaces and times of the history of the human imagination.[6] Rewritten in general form, as the transhistorical analysis of

---

6 See Franco Moretti, *Graphs, Maps, Trees: Abstract Models for Literary History* (Verso, 2005); Wai Chee Dimock, "Planetary Time and Global Transition: 'Context' in Literary Studies," *Common Knowledge* 9.3 (2003): 488–507; and the books *Through Other Continents: American Literature Across Deep Time* (Princeton UP, 2008); and *Shades of the Planet: American Literature as World Literature* (Princeton UP, 2007).

small literary units, or the history of large ones, these concepts could certainly justify non-period-based categories for the academic job list (and thus in turn for the training of graduate students, for the undergraduate curriculum, and so on).

They will (alas!) almost certainly not. The near-total dominance of period at all levels of the literary profession despite the available alternatives suggests how deeply the institution has *imposed* it— however unconscious that imposition may have been. Period is the untheorized ground of the possibility of literary scholarship. And so we live with its limitations and blind spots.

Let us consider some of these at greater length:

1. Even as periodization in its current institutional form codifies period-based literary study as a method, it creates a canonical set of actual periods to use. One can easily enough imagine another group of periods, which would inculcate a radically different historical order. What we call Victorian literature might look quite different from the perspective of a Victorianist than from that of an imaginary scholar of the 1850–1950 period; if one scholar of each type were in a department, the way the literature of the Victorian period were taught (and oriented toward history) might be quite different, depending on whose class one was in. But we don't know what such a department would look like, because British 1850–1950 is not an MLA job category. Victorian literature is thus read almost exclusively within the framework of its period-concept (1830–1900), or within the history of that period-concept as captured in the history of its scholarship. The point is not that periodization is in and of itself limiting (though it is), but also that the current configuration of periods constitutes on the inside of the concept a canon of appropriate use.

2. Periods as we use them, even as they theorize the logic of a chronological whole, presume geographic limits. These are almost

always national. Again, "Victorian" comes to our aid: why should French or Spanish literature contain a "Victorian" period? The question is absurd; but comparing the content and connotations of, say, the "Mid-Victorian" and "Second Empire" periods evokes much more difference than identity. To be against periodization is thus also to be against the dominance of national concepts in the study of literature (and therefore the institutionalization of that dominance in national-language departments). Here again the point is not that geographic limits are in and of themselves bad—the period discussed in part 2, modernity, though not a period-based job category in literature, has geographic limits too—but that the actual dominance of periodization in the literary academy today carries in its wake, and justifies, a strong bias toward national limits, and national limits only.

3. Periods instantiate more or less untheorized and inherited notions of totality. Insofar as periods are definitions, they conceptualize themselves as the product of a set of central characteristics and deviations from them. In general, no matter how extensive the deviations are, the central concept or inner essence governing the period remains firmly in place. The ongoing dominance of a core version of modernism, relentlessly unmodified by the arrival of previously noncanonical authors from a variety of national and social locations, offers us a fairly clear example of how that process works in practice—even when most scholars agree that these new noncanonical authors *should* alter the core meaning of modernism! But more generally we need to be suspicious of how periods do not just "secretly imply or project narratives or 'stories,'" but do so in relation to a larger "historical sequence in which such individual periods take their place and from which they derive their significance."[7]

---

7 Fredric Jameson, *The Political Unconscious: Narrative as a Socially Symbolic Act* (Cornell UP, 1981), 28; on this same subject, see chapter 2 of Jameson, *A Singular Modernity: Essay on the Ontology of the Present* (Verso, 2002), 23–30.

This remark of Jameson's directs us to the ways any single period theorizes an entire apparatus or background against which its own essence emerges, and thus allows us to grasp the dually totalizing nature of periodization, which operates both as an inward-directed theory or typology of wholeness or essentiality, and as an outward-directed presumption about the historical bed that hosts or incubates, at regular intervals, those types of wholeness. It is perhaps because the latter aspect of this dialectic operates in some respects "outside" the realm of the period as such that it does not have much impact on most contemporary scholarship that operates under its aegis. For the limited impact of the former, which ought if nothing else to inculcate a serious and ongoing suspicion of the nature of the concept at the heart of period-based work, we have fewer excuses.

4. Insofar as periods instantiate logics of totality, they instantiate fairly unsophisticated ones. That is, period logics are not only largely untheorized as units of historical significance, they're not very interesting when you do theorize them. Most periods rely on a theory of origins (the mode or tone of the period is grasped, darkly), development (it is carried forward; a spirit emerges), peaks (it achieves one or more high points), declines (it appears in a late, "high" version, beginning of the end), supersessions (it struggles to maintain energy, achieves a decadent version of itself), and ghostly returns (its spirit emerges, a generation or two later, in an ironic, revolutionary, or nostalgic mode). In so doing they place at their center the concepts of originality, development, and belatedness that lie at the center of the "modern" world-view. As I suggested in the preface, the dominance of this view for concepts of period tends to narrate the history of the aesthetic in European time, emplotting beginnings, middles, and ends in a manner that is not, as Hayden White suggested four decades ago, merely neutral.[8]

---

8 Hayden White, *Metahistory: The Historical Imagination in Nineteenth-Century Europe* (Johns Hopkins UP, 1974).

5. Periods (as instituted) codify an unstated theory of how periodization works in historical time. Periods get shorter as we get closer to the present; they expand as we move backward. Why? Is this compression a pragmatic response to historical increases in density of information? A scholar of Jurassic literature has less to read than a scholar of the eighteenth century (*pace* David Hildebrand Wilson); the latter period must be shorter, so that people have time to get to know the canon. It would be strange to have organized our entire discipline around a limitation governed by how much time we have to read, but if that's what we've done, we ought to say so. If that's not it, what else? Do periods get shorter because something changes in the nature of historical time? Do we believe that increases in information density or rates of technological change produce more frequent alterations in the nature of historical totalities, so that the era-concepts periods name replace one another more quickly as we approach the present? Maybe we do, though I doubt it, since no one seems to feel the need to make the case.[9] It is more likely that these units of time, which all appear under the name of "period," name units of a "different species."[10] This leads

9 Someone says: the shortening of periods is an effect of something in the world, namely the increased production of relevant information, and not an arbitrary imposition on humanist grounds. Reply: but the imposition is arbitrary (historically speaking) insofar as it is an effect generated by a preexisting theory of how much information can be consumed in the appropriate institutional time frame, which determines the very *nature* of the period-concept. It is emphatically not the result of a coherent theory of the historical relation between periodicity (as a concept, or as a fact of history—someone would have to make the case either way) and information density. If you say something like "new periods have to be shorter, because there's so much information that no one can master them," what you mean is that "no one can master them *as a period*"—which begs the question.

10 The phrase is from Claude Lévi-Strauss, who writes, "It is thus not only fallacious but contradictory to conceive of the historical process as a continuous development, beginning with prehistory coded in tens or hundreds of millennia, then adopting the scale of millennia when it gets to the 4th or 3rd millennium, and continuing as history in centuries interlarded, at the pleasure of each author, with slices of annual history within the century, day to day history within the year or even hourly history within a day.... Each code refers to a system of meaning which is, at least in theory, applicable to the virtual totality of human history" (*The Savage Mind* [U of Chicago P, 1966], 260).

inexorably to the least flattering possibility: that the decreasing size of periods is an effect of chronological narcissism, of our self-regard for the moment of our historical present, in which the receding and foreshortened past plays Kansas to our Manhattans.[11] What should we do, if the entire literary profession is built on that? I don't know, and you don't know either, since no one asks the question.[12]

6. Periodizing scholarship promotes historical microscopism, in which the place of original scholarship (and hence advanced work) appears only at the highest levels of historical magnification. Nowhere is this clearer than the undergraduate curriculum in the humanities, which moves almost invariably from the large survey of a vast swath of literary or historical space and time—often taught, in large universities, by adjuncts or graduate students—to the narrowly focused senior seminar, in which advanced students, having earned the right to specialize in the craft production of barns in nineteenth-century Pennsylvania, learn under the guidance of a tenure-line faculty member.[13] The entire curriculum thus suggests that large periods and regions—world history, the British survey, introduction to the literature of the Americas—are to be studied by novices, who must earn the right to approach the professional

11 As in the Saul Steinberg cartoon on the cover of the *New Yorker* on March 29, 1976, which shows a foreshortened view of the United States as seen from 9th Avenue. Manhattan's far West side takes up the bottom half of the image, the rest of the continent the next third, and the Pacific Ocean the next fifth; East Asia appears as a distant group of flattened lumps, and the rest of the world fades into sky and the masthead.

12 One of the major effects of this habit on the existing system is, however, that earlier periods, which tend to cover far longer swaths of time, tend to be less nationally and linguistically singular than later ones—see medieval studies or classics. Presumably the scholar of Jurassic literature would likewise be responsible for the literature of more than one species of dinosaur.

13 That the craft production of barns in nineteenth-century Pennsylvania will turn out, in the seminar, to be the nexus of a wide variety of historical effects, and thus become a convex mirror of its age, almost goes without saying. The theory of history that makes such a revelation possible resembles the theory of meaning that undergirds the writing of a major genre of popular history ("the spice/fireplace instrument/sneeze/equation that changed the world"), as well as the epistemology of close reading.

by passing through a series of concentric, periodizing circles: from world history to modern history, from modern history to U.S. history, U.S. history to the history of the Civil War, and from the Civil War to a senior seminar featuring a field trip to Gettysburg. Only in the last two of these smaller circles do the categories governing the professional job lists (in history departments as in literature), or the active scholarship of the faculty, begin to appear.

Among the things that get lost in such a system is the actual historical power of a category like "modernity," which disappears almost entirely by the time you get to the study of 1863. The degree to which such a disappearance seems natural, and subtends a completely unconscious theory of historical relevance, was made especially clear to me a few years ago when, hearing me propose that senior seminars on the literature of 1863 be replaced occasionally by senior seminars on the literature of modernity, a friend of mine asked, "But what about historical context?" Hal, I replied, modernity *is* a historical context. That it doesn't *feel* like one is the result of the way we think about periods.

The problem with microscopism, as with indeed all of the limitations period imposes, is not that it inherently produces bad scholarship. The problem is that the structural relationship between the particular and the general produced by these limitations encourages certain kinds of questions and certain kinds of answers, and discourages or makes impossible others. Because we do not train students to ask questions about large historical periods, for instance, we produce students who in general do not ask such questions. In literature and history, this creates an odd effect on the trajectory of scholarly careers, in which it takes most scholars until their third books to approach large historical or trans-periodizing categories. But this means that such categories will tend to get addressed only by people who write three or more books—a tiny minority of the profession. The end result is that the system reproduces itself, which

is of course what systems do, but: too neatly. The institutionalization of periods does not need to include the institutionalization of
periodization.

The students know this. According to Jennifer Summit, a 2008–9
exercise to revise the English major at Stanford University produced
complaints from students that though their individual courses were
plenty interesting, students lacked "a big picture that would supply
connections between and across their classes: they confirmed what
many of us have long perceived and lamented, that they lack a basic
grid of historical knowledge that could give broader perspective and
unity to their individual classes. Repeatedly, they told us that they
felt the absence of an arc in which their classes could fit together."[14]
This is the result of the fracturing of knowledge into forms of historical specialization that act as alibis for ignorance; the process reifies
a sense that the only context that ever matters is the most local or
historically immediate one. But who is to say that what happened
on June 27, 1914, has *more to do* with the assassination of Archduke
Ferdinand than the history of capitalism? And who is to say that the
historicity of that assassination is best collected or gathered—in a
philosophical sense—in the precise moment of its occurrence, as
though any given instant were a bottomless well of gathered significance, including all possible frames of its analysis? (What theory of
the instant grounds that latter claim?) The "basic grid of historical
knowledge" that would contextualize such an event for a lay audience needs also to be the subject of our most scholarly analyses.
Instead it is an encyclopedia article we pass through, and "beyond,"
in our production of publishable professional knowledge.

14 Summit, "Literary History and the Curriculum," 143.

Chapter 11

Institutional Problems Require
Institutional Solutions

What to do? Alternatives to the structure we have now can be minimally imagined by simply reversing or altering the forms of constraint (and possibility) that govern the periods (and theory of periods) we have. These alternative periods would each constitute, as our periods do now, a *tertium quid*, the "third thing" that, held stable, justifies the act of description and comparison.[1] Here then are four ways to create new periods, none of which requires abandoning the basic premises of period-based history, no matter how limiting those are:[2]

1. Conceive periods organized around times (either arbitrary, like 1850–1950, or conceptual, like the Enlightenment) that cross or combine our existing ones.

---

1 It is because they are both "modernists," arguably, that we can easily discuss Hemingway and Woolf together; the word *modernist*, which is in effect *held still* in the act of comparison, allows for differences to become meaningful against a background of artificial and contingent similarity. Hemingway and Dante would require a different *tertium*.

2 Here Walter Benjamin's remark that the "concept of mankind's historical progress cannot be sundered from the concept of its progression through a homogeneous, empty time" invites us to consider how the putative temporal rupture created by the period boundary operates *within* a commonsense framework of historical movement. That is why periodization cannot recognize what Benjamin calls the "leap in the open air of history" that is the dialectic—and why the theory of the between-period rupture must be understood as part of, and not an exception to, the notion of the period (Benjamin, "On the Concept of History," *Selected Writings*, vol. 4 *1938–1940*, ed. Howard Eiland and Michael Jennings [Harvard UP, 2003], 394–95).

2. Develop periods specifically designed to cross national boundaries. These would borrow for their logic some non-national principle of social or cultural coherence, generating concepts like systems literature, literature of various economic formations (capitalism, feudalism, industrialism), literature of the city-state period, literature of Golden Ages, all of which would join medieval literature in this category.[3]

3. Imagine periods as they might look from some moment other than the present (thereby at least attempting to mitigate chronocentrism). What scholars in the United States and United Kingdom call modernism will surely not exist as a period of literary specialization in the Robot University of the Future™, from which it will be as historically distant as we are from the early modern. What happens if we conceive of modernism as lying at the historical midpoint of a longer period that includes it? Or as lying at the beginning, or end, of a longer period that begins or ends with it? What would such a period be called? What kinds of work would find themselves umbrellaed by such a concept?

4. Support periods using telescopic models that lead from the small to the large, rather than the reverse. In such a curriculum students might begin with a large first-semester lecture course on a single year before earning, in the senior year, the right to ask the really big important questions, like ones about the culture of the second millennium. How would such

---

3 Two recent models from comparative East Asian studies, in which "court" and "empire" serve as *tertia* and organizing chronotopes, are, respectively, David R. Knechtges and Eugene Vance, eds., *Rhetoric and the Discourses of Power in Court Culture: China, Europe, and Japan* (U of Washington P, 2005); and Fritz-Heiner Mutschler and Achim Mittag, eds., *Conceiving the Empire: China and Rome Compared* (Oxford UP, 2009). Tellingly, both books are collections of essays, with the comparisons coming, as a result, mostly between essays rather than inside them.

students learn to think? What sorts of pedagogical and critical mechanisms would train and develop those kinds of thought, or integrate them into what we already know? What if departments included scholars trained in both sorts of approaches, who would be forced to be at least partially responsible to the evidentiary and argumentative norms of their colleagues?

The projects emerging from these new periods are easy enough to imagine. What we need most are examples of how to do them, which means that we need to become more open to experimental forms of scholarship, perhaps especially when such scholarship comes from graduate students and junior faculty, who tend, by virtue of the pressures of the job market, to be the site for the (frequently reluctant) articulation of the profession's most conformist institutionalizations.[4]

This book, needless to say, aims to provide one example of what experimentation in literary history would look like. The variables and the modes operate at the intersection of a number of different concerns and relations to the study of literature. The notion of aesthetic worldedness, as well as the variables that govern it, both developed in part 1, are essentially transhistorical or even ahistorical analytic categories designed to draw attention to a feature of the artwork (its "world") and some ways that we can observe its alterations.[5] The

4 Urging people to play it safe, usually for their own good, produces a profession full of people trained out of their most experimental impulses. Fear of the conservatism of imaginary others (in hiring, publishing, or tenure decisions) thus becomes the primary value governing professional development: don't do X, even though I think it's a good idea, because I'm worried that some conservative people (who may or may not exist) will punish you for doing X.

5 Like everything else the variables should be historicized, but whatever in them remained recognizable over the course of historical change—whatever allowed one to recognize dynamism in historical situation A as substantially the same as dynamism in historical situation B—would be the *tertium quid*, just as in the history of the novel the thing called "novel" is held steadily enough to allow for the consideration of its historical variations within a single frame.

system of modes that appears in part 2 tracks the system or structure governing the actual shapes of aesthetic worldedness in a single social mode (which overlaps, obviously, with the historical period that bears its name). Insofar as the analysis is of modernity, it owes something to the logic of historical periods or eras that undergirds the periodization model. Because it describes the history of the modern work of art as the effect of a set of structural relationships, however, the analysis avoids the progressive and developmental habits that operate normatively inside current periodization theory. As I suggest in the final appendix, the choice of any given period as a frame for a discussion of Realism, Romanticism, and Modernism is essentially arbitrary. Smaller or larger periods would generate their own histories of relations among the modes. The logic of Realism, Romanticism, and Modernism thus does not belong to the modern period proper (though the names given those relationships do). "Modernity" is just one of many possible scales of analysis. What matters is how history is handled inside the period concept; or rather, what function the period concept *serves* in an overarching methodological structure oriented around the synchronic or the systematic (because the period, despite its appeal to diachronism across period boundaries, operates inside them as a static, epochal principle).[6]

Among the effects on the literary institution of an imaginary, wholescale adoption of the terms in the first two parts of this book would be the development of some new kinds of scholarship. One can imagine, for instance, scholars focused largely on one or another configuration of the variables or modes: someone interested in shifts from Romantic to Realist dominance in justifications of the impulse to creation; someone who mainly studies the modes in relation to diegetic geographies; someone who applies the modes or

6 These remarks echo comments made by Roman Jakobson and Jurij Tynjanov in "Problems in the Study of Literature and Language" (1928), in *Readings in Russian Poetics*, ed. Ladislav Matejka and Krystyna Pomorska (Dalkey Archive, 2002).

variables to nonfictional genres (documentaries, criticism); some-one who parses the differences between British and American liter-ary modernism by contrasting the modal location of the Modernist impulse to cacography (denotative in the former; often connotative in the latter); someone who thinks through the history of residual forms across major shifts in world-view, and thus studies the history of lyric in the modern.

Each of these practices could be pursued across a variety of geographic, historical, and aesthetic fields. Their effects would be, among other things, to cut the pie of literary history in new and hopefully interesting ways. On such a pie, objects formerly located on different slices might turn out to be contiguous (in a square located at the exact center of the pie, e.g.), while formerly proximate ones might belong instead to opposing categories. A fully reimagined pie might end up with pieces resembling gerry-mandered Congressional districts, or, if one allowed the carving knife to move on the horizontal axis, open itself up to three-di-mensional topologies. Such new juxtapositions, separations, and proximities could usefully contrast, by providing us with other models of literary history and literary likeness, the habits of our current methods. The goal is finally not to have one way to cut the pie, but many.

Here in this book, then, the lesson is that certain theories of his-tory may allow us to alter periodizing models from the inside, as it were, not by challenging their boundaries but by changing the kinds of historical thought that operate them. My chosen methods have been the flexible structuralism governing the relationships between the modes and the typology of the analysis of literary worlds. These take their place among a number of other actually existing models for considering historical action outside the teleology of periods. Such other ways of thinking include the *longue durée* approach of the Annales school (finding its purchase in literary studies now in the sudden, occasionally alarming popularity of world-systems theory), the Marxist dialectic, or, more speculatively, concepts like Derrida's *hauntology* (which is, in some respects, the application of the logic of individual memory developed by Freud to the historical sphere), or Badiou's *event*.[7]

The obvious intellectual attractions of these models (and others) at the level of individual scholarship and thought contrasts depressingly, however, with their collective institutional impotence, their incapacity to alter the system within which these works are read and taught. But of course this is not surprising: institutional problems require *institutional* solutions. The challenge is not to describe or challenge commonsense theories of historicity; it is to develop structures that encode our resistance to them. Meeting such a challenge will require new curricula and new measures of competence or intellectual legitimacy at both the undergraduate and graduate levels. Things like the traditional comprehensive exam, organized so often around the period-based job field, would not be an appropriate measure for students attempting dissertations on the history of the epic imagination. Training students to think well about highly transnational and transperiodizing concepts like the modern, or (psst!) the dramatic aside, or teaching them to develop structuralist or *longue durée* models of analysis, would require letting go of our current sense that in-depth knowledge can come only through the mastery of a restricted, period-oriented canon of works. We would instead have to develop ways to teach students how to produce new knowledge about such concepts within the framework of existing curricular structures; or, more likely, we would have to modify our curricula to suit those new methods.

7   None of these is without its problems; for a critique of the Annales approach, see Jacques Rancière, *The Names of History: On the Poetics of Knowledge*, trans. Hassan Melehy (U of Minnesota P, 1994). But a diversity of concepts inoculates the institution against the limits of any single approach. On hauntology, see Jacques Derrida, *Specters of Marx*, trans. Peggy Kamuf (Routledge, 1994); on the event, see Alain Badiou, *Being and Event*, trans. Oliver Feltham (Continuum, 2007).

What would it take to train a graduate student (in the usual five to ten years) to do original scholarship informed by any of these proposed periods or methods (Enlightenment literature, the history of the literary syllogism)? What kinds of goals would we set ourselves when teaching undergraduates; what kind—or rather, what *kinds*—of thinkers would we be aiming to help create? What would happen to the life of a literary studies department, should there be any left at the Robot University, should some of its students and faculty be trained in new periods or transperiodizing concepts, and others in the traditional period-based models? What would it be like to work in a university that had codified such differences in its curricula, its graduate exams, or its hiring practices?

I don't know, and I would like to know. If you are, like me, in a position to write and do professionally more or less what you would like, and if you, like me, would like to know, I recommend some minimal first steps. They are, first, to *produce work that creates models* for the kinds of literary historical work we hope to institutionalize in the curriculum and especially in the training of graduate students (all very well for me to write a book on literary lists from Sei Shonagon to Georges Perec by way of the venerable Bede; professionally difficult for job seekers to do so, without existing examples of that kind to justify the project); second, to *stop advertising and hiring exclusively in period-based job categories*; and third, to *reshape the undergraduate and graduate curricula* in ways that undermine the assumption that our current model of periodization is the natural frame for literary study. These three changes, each simple enough in its own way (and listed here in increasing order of institutional difficulty), would go some distance toward bringing to light the theories of history that we have allowed unconsciously and materially to dominate the work we do.

* * *

Why bother?

Not only, though I confess to a certain personal curiosity regarding the effects of looking at the world from new angles, because these institutional changes give us new things to think about and new work to do. But because the way things are now damages the world in two ways. First, it eliminates certain kinds of thinking from professional consideration, thereby interfering with the twin projects of Enlightenment thought—still worth believing in!—to speak well and truthfully about the world, and to consider in as serious a way as possible the role one's own truth-procedures play in that speaking. Second, the institutionalization of periodization reinforces a presentist and dissociative form of historical thinking that makes the world a less good, more stupid place to live in. The claim that periodization is presentist might seem on its face paradoxical, for one of the claims made for conventional period studies is that it allows for deep specialization in a bounded historical (and by implication geographical) field. But the consequence of such specialization as it is often practiced is to cut the past off from the present, to privilege a way of imagining the past that itself completely in the past, without interest in—or even knowledge of—that past's future, which is our present. The position that the past is irrelevant to the present, which offers its holder the substantial advantage of not needing to think or read about anything before five minutes ago, belongs both to the belligerent anti-scientism and fantasies of strict constructionism motivating the worst demons of contemporary U.S. political life. It also exacerbates a more general sense that the present *as a period* owes its historical specialness to its capacity to continually shrug off even its most recent past, in the form of another concluded and irrelevant period. Such thinking grants the present a kind of protected historical and epistemological status, in which only evidence from the era immediately before one's eyes— which is to say the first set of things one thinks or feels, developed with no sense of their relation to any other thinking or feeling done elsewhere or elsewhen—counts as relevant for making judgments that, in turn, will five minutes from now belong to the tenebrating crepuscule of the distant past. The strange shrinkage of periodization as it extends toward the present, reinforced now in the recent academic interest in the "contemporary" as a critical category, must therefore be understood in part as a reaction to (and dismissal of) the increasing evidence we have that our present births itself from forms of historical causality borne of far longer, even inhuman periodizations—among them capitalism and modernity, to be sure, but also the literally geological factors of climate change and the destiny of the planet.[8]

That periods shorten as they approach us thus affects not only the present but also the future, where it has the effect of making it impossible to imagine any kind of long-term change in the social, political, or environmental conditions of everyday life—as though the everyday or the quotidian, once believed to be a refuge from the grand-narrative politics of the structures of power, had become instead a nightmare vision of the type articulated in *Groundhog Day* or *The Truman Show*, an endless series of repetitions in which no substantive action (except, the movies tell us, love!) can remake the basic social situation in which we live. No wonder, then, that the justificatory claims that "history can tell us about the present,"

8 The tendency to periodize, with its capacity to release the present from the past, remains one of modernity's great gifts to itself; in this respect it is, as Margreta de Grazia has written, only "when the present sees itself as discrete from what preceded it—when it in effect periodizes itself" that "modernity has arrived" ("The Modern Divide: From Either Side," *Journal of Medieval and Early Modern Studies* 37.3 [2007]: 456). It is in this sense that, as Fredric Jameson has written, "we cannot not periodize," though as he goes on to say, such a recognition opens the door for a "thoroughgoing relativization of historical narratives," one that allows us to treat modernity as a trope or story (*A Singular Modernity: Essay on the Ontology of the Present* [Verso, 2002], 29–30). On Jameson's remarks, and for the source of the epigraph to chapter 10, see Margreta de Grazia, "The Modern Divide: From Either Side," *Journal of Medieval and Early Modern Studies* 37.3 (2007): 453–67.

used routinely to substantiate an interest in the dim and distant, ring so emptily these days, even if they are all we have. The words are premised on a sense that history matters by virtue of its allegorical capacity to resemble, with varying opacity, some significant feature of contemporary life—George W. Bush as Louis-Napoléon, the American empire as Rome, and so on. But in such comparisons the game has already been lost, since their kelson is not that we are *still in* the history of the French nineteenth century, but that we are beyond it, and that what we learn from it will only appear to us as an imperfect analogue and treacherous guide. The truth is that the history is shared, temporally and geographically, as far as we allow it to be, and that individual lives can impact its geological forces only when they are taught to recognize that such a potential has at many other moments been an achieved historical fact. Against such a recognition, the institutionalization of periodization keeps us safe from history, and keeps history, in turn, safe from us.

PART IV

APPENDIXES

APPENDIXES

Chapter 12

The Empty Quadrant

A recent conversation with Jos Lavery opened onto the possibility of a fourth quadrant in the matrix defining the modal responses to any dominant world-view.

That empty square, which would be the paradoxical site of an acceptance of the world and a refusal of the world-question, would be there where the work attempted to escape the demand to meditate on or even recognize the terms of representation, while nonetheless continuing to represent the world as such.

Though any object that emerged as a work could only ever partially occupy such a position, it may be useful to understand the meaning of the empty quadrant by imagining the kind of impossibility a fully committed work of its type would aim for, and comparing it to the varieties of impossibility and invisibility mandated by the purest versions of the other three. To review: a purely Realist work would be *indistinguishable* from ordinary life (its affirmation would merge with the general affirmation of the common state of affairs); a purely Romantic work would be *inaccessible* to ordinary life (its imaginary new world would have no cognitive aperture);

	Yes to the world-concept	*No* to the world-concept
Yes to the world	Realism (affirmation)	*The empty quadrant*
No to the world	Romanticism (creation-destruction)	Modernism (refusal)

and a purely Modernist work would be *incomprehensible* to ordinary life (its refusal would extend to the very possibility of communication). In each case the extension of a logic to its extreme produces the total illegibility of the art work as such, and traces the asymptote of a certain aesthetic ambition.

As for the empty quadrant, which affirms the terms of the question but refuses to offer an answer, perhaps it would approach the realm of the arbitrary and the indifferent. At its near-limit that indifference (of the work to, among other things, the notion of the work) would produce a merger of the work and the world. The work would be indifferent to the world, and to itself as work; it would appear as intentionlessness, as randomness, as an accidental collocation. At the pure limit we would read the work as nonwork, as chance or happenstance, or as the result of a passive and entirely unmotivated recording device (as one reads, for instance, the stone's part in tracing the outline of a fossil). Sliding down the asymptote toward legibility one might reach a work that remained in place long enough for the recording, indicative act to be observed, in which a kind of glimpse, an eddy, in the fabric of the real would suffice to suggest a perspective on existing circumstances that would be an act of reading, making, or recognition. The slight disturbance or residue of such an act of making would signal, at the limit, the encounter between the Romantic, creative mode and the theoretically empty activity of the mode belonging to the empty quadrant.

The aesthetic that comes most readily to mind for such a mode is Roland Barthes's "neutral," whose relation to both politics and the aesthetic attempts to negate the demand that the work take a position in relation to the field of its appearance.[1] In an e-mail Jos

---

1 Roland Barthes, *The Neutral: Lecture Course at the College de France (1977–1978)*, trans. Rosalind Kraus and Denis Hollier (Columbia UP, 2007); see also the discussion of his essay "Alors, la Chine?" in Eric Hayot, *Chinese Dreams: Pound, Brecht, Tel quel* (U of Michigan P, 2003).

suggests Oscar Wilde, Christina Rossetti, Jacques Derrida, Kathy Acker, John Ashbery. I wonder also if this mode might not include some of the work that emerges from the stricter limitations and forms of arbitrary constraint used by writers of the Oulipo group; I am particularly thinking of something like Georges Perec's pseudo-journalistic experiments in *Espèces d'espaces*, or of the appearance, a millennium from now, of the highly radiation-resistant bacterium *Deinococcus radiodurans*, whose DNA has been rewritten into poetry by Christian Bök;[2] and of course Walter Benjamin's *Arcades Project*. Whether the lists in Sei Shōnagon's *Pillow Book* qualify here would have to be determined by an analysis of their relation to the general world-view of eleventh-century Japan.

2 See Christian Bök, "The Xenotext Experiment" *SCRIPTed* 5.2 (2008), www.law. ed.ac.uk/ahrc/script-ed/vol5–2/editorial.asp.

Chapter 13

Medium and Form

"Don't be a diegetic positivist!" This rallying cry (so often heard at the barricades in 1968!) came to me from a reader of the book's first two parts. If world is, as I assert in part 1, the totality of the diegesis, and no more, this is so in order to retain the force of the *literal* application of "world" to the work, which guarantees (and is guaranteed in turn by) the analysis of part 2. In another book, or with different ambitions, one might well have said, the world is a model of totality, as the work is a model of totality, and so no need to constrain oneself to the diegesis—which is, I think, what Jean-Luc Nancy essentially believes. From such a perspective "world" would be fundamentally metaphorical, and my use of it to refer solely to the diegetic totality constituted by the work an extravagant limitation on the theory of worldedness developed here, a too-literal investment in the concept of the world producing a concomitant underinvestment in the notion of totality as a function of the entirety of the work of art—an entirety that includes, among other things, two undeniable exteriors to the aesthetic diegesis, medium and form. A complete analysis of world-variables and -modes would, therefore, have to bring the whole work under its project or program.

The undeniable appeal of such a position should not obscure the fact that it is wrong. It is wrong specifically in its failure to grasp that the representational function of the diegesis of the work is, most crucially, an aspect of its form. The diegetic totality has, insofar as it is diegetic and insofar as it is total, a privileged relation to worldedness that stems exactly from its literal appeal to the world as concept. To suggest that the "world" that emerges from the diegetic whole is just one part of the general conceptual worldedness of the work as a totality is to confuse "totality" and "world," which, though they resemble each other, are after all not quite the same thing. The diegesis-creating work of art is, among other things, a theory of totality *as* world. It is in this quite literal reference to and theorization of the world as theme that the aesthetic diegesis achieves its figuration of world as form.

Understanding things this way has the advantage of making it possible to describe in a clearer way how both medium and form participate in the production or apprehension of diegetic space. That description in turn helps to affirm the vital importance of those categories for the long-run analysis of the history of literary worlds.

Medium: the narrative on cell phone is not the narrative in codex; the narrative novelized is not the narrative illustrated, or fanned in epic iambs. In each case medium, the haptic, phenomenological interface between a work and its apprehension by a subject makes its effects felt in spatiotemporal terms. The varieties of extension appropriate to the visual or the narrative work were typologized, in Lessing's *Laocoön*, as differences between spatial (painting, sculpture) and temporal (literature) experiences of the aesthetic. Joseph Frank has argued, in his work on spatial form, that modernist literature was novel at least in part because it attempted to break the habits Lessing described, blocking the graduated apprehensions of ordinary narrative in order to unleash the meaning of the whole in a single synchronic gesture of quasi-pictorial enlightenment.[1] These broad strokes suggest the beginnings of a theory of medium-worlds, each the phenomenological situation constituted

---

1 Gotthold Ephraim Lessing, *Laocoön: An Essay on the Limits of Painting and Poetry*, trans. Edward Allen McCormick (Johns Hopkins UP, 2004); Joseph Frank, *The Idea of Spatial Form* (Rutgers UP, 1991).

by a work's consumption (trance of the private reading of a novel at home; hiccupping stimulus of text messages read on the subway; unfolding of the fading snapshot from a wallet or purse; public meditation on the museum image, or applause for the theatrical spectacle).[2] Each of these experiences gives us a different arrangement of space and time, not only in the encounter between viewer and artwork but also in the locatedness of that encounter within a larger public sphere that includes the viewer's awareness of the broad patterns of consumption a medium encourages and defines. Thus the fabled solitude of the consumption of codex novels takes place within an awareness that, in reading alone, one reads like others reading alone, just as the seat in the theater on some single night means witnessing a performance that one knows will never be repeated in exactly this way. The world-creating force of medium emerges from the dialectic between the *pattern* of individual experiences a given medium creates and, because "technical factors cannot [alone] create a style," the mood and action of the work whose consumption the medium permits.[3]

How, then, to relate that consumptional worldedness to the diegetic action of the representational capacity of the work—to read the totality of the work as including both the diegetic world and the one made by its medium? Interpretively, the trick would be to figure out how, or whether, we could describe certain effects of the

2 The discussion that proceeds from here is esoteric. But for a simple illustration of the effects of medium on diegesis, consider that both Thomas Pavel and Gérard Genette argue that the "density" (for Pavel) or "speed" (for Genette) of a novel depends quite simply on the relation between action and the number of physical pages (or words) in a book (Pavel, *Fictional Worlds* [Harvard UP, 1986], 100; Genette, *Narrative Discourse: An Essay in Method*, trans. Jane E. Lewin [Cornell UP, 1983]).

3 Heinrich Wölfflin, *Renaissance and Baroque*, trans. Kathrin Simon (Cornell UP, 1964), 79. The relations among media could then additionally be historicized, along the lines, for instance, developed by Jacques Rancière, who suggests that beginning in the nineteenth century the arts themselves become geometrized, collapsing the strict separation between the spatial and the temporal (sculpture and poetry, but also painting and cinema). See Rancière, *The Future of the Image*, trans. Gregory Elliott (Verso, 2007).

medium-world as relating (in ways that matter) to the effects of the diegetic one. This is not simply a question of looking at works that strongly activate medium-effects (Antonioni's *Blow Up*, Phillips's *A Humument*) and showing that the diegesis makes us think about the medium. Such an analysis does not activate the world-concept. To do so, one would have to establish a relationship between the phenomenological world of the medium's consumption and the diegetic world—rubbing, for instance, the presumptive publicity and transitoriness of the experience of reading a cell phone novel against the nature of the public and the transitory in the diegetic world itself (these parsed, potentially, as features of amplitude and dynamism). The relation between these two worlds could then be mapped on to the modes, so that theory of the "total" world of the work—including both medium and diegesis—could appear. I have to say that an analysis of this sort seems like it would be quite difficult to accomplish, which does not mean it is not worth trying.[4]

Form is easier. It points more firmly toward the diegesis. If we consider the latter to describe not simply representational space, but indeed any "interior" space generated by the work of art, then we can think of form as the structure governing the horizons of the diegetic world. Those horizons can be, as in the novel or in landscape painting, highly mimetic; they can be, as in certain kinds of abstract art, in lyric poetry or theater, especially in non-Western classical

---

4 Because developments in aesthetic media are tightly connected to the introduction of new technologies, the danger is that we read mediatic change as progress toward a phenomenological or worldly ideal (as figured, for instance, in virtual reality or the *Gesamtkunstwerk*). Against such a tendency, it is useful to think about the ways in which culture chooses, from what one might think of as the "genetic" representational and social capacity of any given medium (the codex, the performance hall, the phonograph, the body), a preferred set of options and structures that come to dominate it. Consider, for instance, the prominence of "actualities" in the early cinema, during a period in which it was not at all clear, as Mary Ann Doane has shown, that narrative would become the dominant mode of cinematic representation, or of the film industry (Doane, *The Emergence of Cinematic Time: Modernity, Contingency, the Archive* [Harvard UP, 2002]).

traditions, primarily emotional; they can be, as sometimes in sound poetry, in dance, or in the cinema, primarily sensory or kinesthetic. Form amounts to restrictions or limits on the nature of possible aesthetic worlds, which are what help make the sonnet a sonnet and the program short story a program short story.[5] If we consider those differences as orientations toward the question of the world, then we must recognize that form, which determines the horizon of a work's world-imagination, is a crucial feature of the general history of world-orientedness. There is a Realism of the sonnet as form—a normative formal world-orientation created by the octave-sestet (higher amplitude), or quatrain-couplet (lower amplitude) structure, its relation to lyric, its historically established patterns of representation, and so on. That formal Realism interacts with the diegetic world produced inside any given sonnet, which may or may not be diegetically Realist in its effects, since these latter must be measured against a world-oriented diegetic norm. A sonnet written in the twentieth century operates in a different standard of diegetic Realism than one written during the fifteenth, even as it obeys, at least roughly, the same formal one. We might say, therefore, of works like Pushkin's *Eugene Onegin* or Vikram Seth's *Golden Gate* that they smash the formal Realism of the sonnet against the diegetic Realism of the novel, and that they resolve that titanic encounter in both diegetic and formal space.

As we see from the example of the sonnet, form is among other things a coalescence of features that amount to a world-relation. Because form endures, it retains, against cultural pressure, a record of world-orientedness that will eventually come to seem—*at the level of form alone*—Romantic or Modernist, thus encoding in the present a "residual" formal memory of another

---

5 On "program" fiction, see Mark McGurl, *The Program Era: Postwar Fiction and the Rise of Creative Writing* (Harvard UP, 2009).

world-view.[6] As much is suggested by the continuing presence of lyric, whose emphasis on diegetic emotion and a bipolar, interpellative relationship between an "I" and a "you," are incompatible, at the formal level, with the major demands of modern diegetic Realism.[7] That lyric survives today, though in a diminished social role, speaks to our need to develop better theories of the ecology of forms at any given historical moment. Carrying over the modes to that project leads me to suggest that there may be a Realism, Romanticism, and Modernism of forms—that there may be, that is, patterns governing formal ecologies that reproduce and rethink at the level of form the world-oriented qualities of diegetic space. A study of the ways in which lyric has adapted, or refused to adapt, its diegetic space to the demands of the modern world-view—or a study of the historical place of lyric in larger formal ecologies— would not simply mirror, presumably, a history of diegetic space in general. Developing the capacity to consider both those histories at the same time—the history of the ecology of form (understood as an arrangement of types and horizons of diegetic space) and the history of diegetic space—would be one crazy endpoint of the project begun here.

6 The entire pantheon of Raymond Williams's descriptions of temporal relations to hegemony—residual, dominant, emergent, preemergent (the "structure of feeling")—can be put to good use in describing the actual social field of forms in any given period, since it allows us to grasp how the present is "lived and practiced on the basis of the residue ... of some previous social and cultural institution or formation" (Williams, *Marxism and Form* [Oxford UP, 1977], 122).

7 The assumption that the lyric organizes at the most basic level an "I" and a "you" is complicated in work (still in manuscript) on the Victorians by my colleague Emily Harrington.

Chapter 14

On the History of Reality

It is impossible not to notice, comparing *Le Morte d'Arthur* (1485) to *Gargantua and Pantagruel* (1532–54) to *Lazarillo de Tormes* (1554), the astonishing difference in the portrayal of reality they provide. From the first pages of *Lazarillo* the reader is in a different world, a fiction, Francisco Rico writes, "governed by the criteria of probability, experience, and common sense, by the same criteria of veracity that are generally used in daily life, and told in language that is in turn substantially in keeping with that of the everyday"—a difference so dramatic in comparison with the basic rules governing the late medieval romance or the Rabelaisian life-world as to constitute a revolution.[1]

A revolution in literary practice, or in life? One of the strange habits of scholarship on the novel and the rise of realism has been the recurring appearance of the feeling that *reality* itself—the basic structures of probability, experience, common sense, and veracity, the mixture of classes, the relation between physics and the metaphysical, between the biological and the social, and so on—remains a constant. This happens even in work that strives to adopt a relativist take on the nature of reality as a historical phenomenon. Take Erich Auerbach's *Mimesis*. There, in the magisterial reading of Dante, with its beautiful descriptions of the sensitivity of the latter's capture of "human reality," of "earthly reality," or of "the history of man's inner life and unfolding," we see Auerbach measuring Dante's

---

1 Francisco Rico, "*Lazarillo de Tormes*," in *The Novel*, vol. 2, "Forms and Themes," ed. Franco Moretti [Princeton UP, 2007], 146.

accomplishment against a stable, consistent notion of human and earthly life, one as knowable in fourteenth-century Verona as it was in twentieth-century Istanbul. Despite Auerbach's debt to Vico, which permits him to historicize the *representation* of reality as a function of human social and intellectual life, he draws the line at reality itself. That same stable notion of reality justifies Auerbach's later remarks on Virginia Woolf: "most of the other novels which employ multiple reflection of consciousness also leave the reader with an impression of hopelessness. There is often something confusing, something hazy about them, something hostile to the reality which they represent."[2] It's specifically the equation of haziness with hostility to reality—a sense that to be hostile to a represented reality means making the work "hazy" or "confusing," making it less representationally accurate in some respects—that represents (and requires) a sense of reality as something that the work either represents, or fails to.

A page later on, however, Auerbach seems to be thinking differently, wondering if Woolf's style isn't the harbinger of a fully new kind of reality governed by "unification and simplification" (553). Is it possible that the basic "human" nature of reality can change? I am not speaking here of some reality so fixed and structural that it will continue to be long after we are all dead, but of the deepest possible nature of a socially constructed version of the actually real, a level of thought only barely accessible to human cognition, but nonetheless capable of geologic or epochal transformations, of operations at inhuman speeds and scales, that would ground the very fabric of human worldedness. Does Auerbach believe that such a reality is subject to historical change? Yes. But also, no.

What to make of this contradiction? Let us compare Auerbach to another critic of roughly the same period. In *The Gates of Horn* Harry

---

2 Erich Auerbach, *Mimesis: The Representation of Reality in Western Literature*, trans. Willard R. Trask (Princeton UP, 2003), 551. Further references in the text.

Levin on several occasions seems to insist on the historical nature of reality itself, writing, for instance, that "the novel, by historical definition, tends to pursue the real—an unending quest, since the object changes its appearance in differing contexts and to different observers."[3] But such statements are mixed in together with others that suggest quite different kinds of theories of the relation between reality and realism. Immediately following the sentence I've just cited, as though providing evidence for it, Levin cites Fernand Léger: "Every epoch has its own realism, invented more or less in relation to the preceding epochs." But that sentence is agnostic on the reality of realism; all you need to say what it says is a belief that aesthetic modes alter themselves in relation to the dominant versions that precede them. Whether reality itself changes (as Levin suggests in his sentence, when he calls it "the real") is not something Léger helps us decide. Some pages later, when Levin writes (of the French new novel) that "all the cinematographic contrivance of *La Jalousie* leaves us farther away from a human relationship than the baffled jealousy of Marcel over Albertine," one feels closer to Auerbach on Dante: the phrase "human relationship" expresses a theory of natural reality against which Robbe-Grillet is found wanting (464). And yet, a page later, Levin, in the space of a single sentence, seems to return to a more historicist position: "the novel, we say, has consistently moved in a realistic direction [does 'realistic' mean toward reality or toward realism? English morphology allows for a temporary ambiguity, resolved following the colon]: in other words, closer and closer to reality." Closer to reality: definitive enough, until the sentence's final clause emerges to put everything back into question: "as continually reinterpreted with reference to a changing style of life and view of the world" (465). Are things settled? Not really. The word

---

3 Harry Levin, *The Gates of Horn: A Study of Five French Realists* (Oxford UP, 1966), 446, my emphasis. Further references in the text.

reinterpreted seems to undermine the certainties of "closer and closer to reality," since no claim is made as to the transformation of the thing being interpreted. Levin is echoing Léger, when a word like *remade* or *transformed* would have left him on more forceful ground.[4]

I take the ambiguities and apparent contradictions in both these cases to be symptoms of a larger problem involving the theorization of reality, and in particular reality's relation to history. We are not faced, in other words, with a situation of carelessness or of ideological blindness, but with the difficulties provoked by the internal inconsistencies and intellectual problems created by historicism itself. To historicize the critic must maintain some stable figure for comparison among people of different places and times, the most minimal of which is some combination of genetic resemblance (guaranteed by the fact of common species, "human" reality), and an environmental one (guaranteed by our common inhabitation of this planet, "earthly" reality). As a result it may be best to speak of a *continuous tension* between two opposing tendencies, which often appear side-by-side, as we see in Auerbach and Levin, with the universalizing one acting as a muted but important support for a variety of claims, even as the more theoretically sophisticated, Viconian model drives, at the level of explicit thought, arguments about the changing history of reality unmoored from all but the most minimal genetic or environmental demands.[5] Here we may return to Bakhtin's assertion that the biographical novel's link with historical

4 We may in fact return to the first sentence I cited from Levin to notice that it performs a similar two-step: "the novel, by historical definition, tends to pursue the real—an unending quest, since the object changes its appearance in differing contexts and to different observers." Imagining the sentence without "its appearance" will give you some sense of the moderating effect it has on what might otherwise have been a nearly absolutist claim about the historical nature of the real.

5 Such ambiguities will appear most clearly, I wish to insist on the basis of these citations from Auerbach and Levin (and Bakhtin, in a moment), in writers whose intellect and honesty allow them to perceive the problem, and to grapple, however unconsciously, with it.

time makes it "possible to reflect reality in a more profoundly realistic way"—where "realistic" seems to mean "in concordance with actual reality"—to witness once again the ways in which a naturalizing view will tend to imagine that reality has been waiting there all along, like the sword in the stone, to be taken up in various historicizable ways by the aesthetic.[6]

At some level to say anything else is implausible: surely the seventy-five years between the *Morte d'Arthur* and *Lazarillo de Tormes* (or, closer, the two years that separate *Lazarillo* from the fourth volume of *Gargantua*) did not witness anything like the transformation of the basic principles of daily life that constitute the largely unconscious physical and social laws governing the texts' represented worlds. "The same criteria of veracity that are generally used in daily life" did not get invented in 1553; like other important aspects of reality, including the laws of physics, we imagine it to have an essentially ahistorical nature.

And yet, we feel no compunction arguing, for instance, that differences between the realism of the nineteenth century and the realism of the late twentieth represent substantive changes not only in the modes of literary representation but also in the very modes of reality itself, that the basic social realities of late capitalism are so different from those of a century ago as to constitute a new reality entirely, for which the artwork, a coal-mine canary, is not merely a description but an index. The very theorization of reality as historical (or not) thus seems to be at least partly an effect of the historical period under discussion. When it comes to thinking inside the modern period, any number of scholarly works seem to believe that reality changes, and that such changes are routinely reflected

---

6 Mikhail Bakhtin, "The *Bildungsroman* and Its Significance in the History of Realism: Toward a Historical Typology of the Novel," in *Speech Genres and Other Late Essays*, trans. Vern W. McGee, ed. Caryl Emerson and Michael Holquist (U of Texas P, 1986), 18.

(and anticipated) in fiction. Outside the modern, however, it is far more common to assume that the reality we know today was simply beyond the creative or social capacities, or interests, of societies that did not, or could not, represent it.

Is such a position reasonable? Is it more plausible to say that reality—the deepest level of the social interaction with something permanent and inhuman—itself changes, and that what we witness when looking at the history of diegetic worlds is not (or not only) a transformation in their capacity to reflect reality but also a transformation in the actual nature of the real? To assert the latter would not require us, I think, to say that real life in the age of the Arthurian romance included no tramps or swindlers, or that the laws of physics or biology applied differently there. We do not ask the work of art to reflect *all* reality; we assume that the readers and writers of Arthurian romance (or Sumerian epic) sweated and farted and ached like the rest of us. If one notes, as does Auerbach, that in such societies the "separation of styles"—the reservation for certain low modes (the comic, e.g.) of an embodied social life, and for high ones of the tragic or epic topics of the privileged class—does not allow romance to sweat, as it were, one can then draw a number of conclusions about such a society on that basis. What one describes at that point is a social norm. But one *assumes* that the reality such a social norm fails to capture remains more or less the one we know now, that is, the one captured so presciently by Dante, or more recently by novels in the tradition of the European nineteenth century. To some extent the problem is that we aren't relativist enough; our analyses of "social" reality always assume that such realities are most fundamentally relations to an actual normal or neutral reality that does not change (this reality is normal or neutral in that it is essentially a combination of biology [laws of the species] and environment [laws of physical life]; but it may also include psychology [laws of desire], anthropology [laws of violence and myth], political economy, geography, sociology, etc.). In such a scheme, the social nature of modern realism is that it approaches most closely this normal or neutral reality.

The tendency to assume that, for works written closer to our present, changes in the modes of representation reflect changes in the *nature* of human reality (consider the way people talk about the modernist or the postmodern novel) suggests how strange the modern treatment of the premodern is. Either our reality is the reality that has been real all along—a position that would justify, for instance, Lukács's critique of Zola—or reality changes over time, in which case the realism of the postmodern novel reflects a new social and political reality that differs from the reality of the classically realist one.[7] We currently have things both ways: we generally hold the first position when we consider the nonmodern, and the second one when we consider the modern. Or, as with Auerbach and Levin, we hold both positions at the same time, managing via ambiguity and parataxis nested propositions that expose but do not resolve the contradictions. At its worst and most commonsensical this leads to a progressive theory of reality-*representation* until roughly the nineteenth century (reality stays the same; people get better at representing it), and then a historically variable theory of reality *itself* once that representational acme is achieved. Either such a pattern reflects an argument about the nature of reality as a function of human history, or it's an expression of the rankest Eurocentrism. We ought to figure out which.[8]

7 Georg Lukács, "Narrate or Describe?" in *Writer and Critic, and Other Essays*, trans. Arthur D. Kahn (Grosset & Dunlap, 1971).

8 In case it's the former, a start: the conceptual core of the problem rests on the boundary that it necessarily imagines between the human (available to history) and the inhuman (not). On either side there is no dilemma; the dilemma is where to draw the boundary (and to ask whether the boundary itself can be historicized). A complete understanding of the problem will certainly not lie in the choice to support one or the other of the terms it sets before us, or a particular configuration of the boundary line, but in our recognition that the structure of the terms and the line is itself the answer to a question that we have not yet asked.

Chapter 15

Beyond the Modern

One of the obvious problems with the terms Realism, Romanticism, and Modernism as names for the modes of world-relation rests in their reification as structure of already-existing terms borrowed from the history of modern European literature. The danger is that this reification implies that the fundamental modes of world-relation appear only for the first time in modern Europe.

Nothing could be further from the theoretical truth. Only *theoretical*, because I am not equipped to do the work that would prove it. Nonetheless I want to insist that, theoretically at least, the structuro-logical description of a series of basic responses to a given assertion—affirmation/conceptualization, creation/destruction, negation/refusal, the neutral—will describe responses to any historically normative world-view. This suggests that for any given social whole or spatio-temporal extension (the Song Dynasty; Byzantium; colonial West Africa; Paris in the 1930s) one could describe a pattern of relations following the basic modal structure. In such a social whole, Realism would refer, as it does in the modern world-view, to the affirmation and conceptualization of the normative, socially dominant position; Romanticism to attempts to revise or rewrite it from inside its fundamental ontological premises; and Modernism to the negation of those premises and the radical imagination of life beyond "world" (however the period defines that latter concept). In any one of these situations, what we now call "realism"—that is, the style that corresponds most closely to the normative Realism of the modern period, to which it lends a name—could easily be relegated to a second- or third-rate position in the production of the aesthetic diegesis.[1] It is thus probable that for the majority of human history the capital-R Realist mode has not been lowercase-r realist at all, that the apparent prominence of realism in the arts is simply an effect of the kinds of historical and geographic blindness produced by the frames and lenses of modernity itself.[2] The close association of realism with the novel form (though not necessarily with prose more generally) would thus reconfirm the novel's importance as the codification of the modal dominant of the modern world-view, even as it explained why the novel did not appear earlier—not because the premoderns were unable to invent it, but because the modal structures organizing their dominant world-views were codified in other forms and other media, including the lyric, drama, and nonfiction prose, not to mention other non- or para-literary genres that chafe at the definitional restrictions of the word *literature* (文,

1 For now, however, the dominance of realism as a literary-critical (and political) ideal shapes the tendency of scholars to justify certain kinds of nonnormative literary activity—either Romantic or Modernist—by suggesting that it represents a deeper realism (and hence, in modernity, Realism). So the gaps and incomprehensibilities of Toni Morrison represent the actually aporetic nature of the African American social experience; likewise the Romantic and "unrealistic" melodrama of Bollywood cinema is taken (rightly) as expressing political realities experienced by its audiences (see Priya Joshi, "Bollylite in America," *South Asian Popular Culture* 8.3 [2010]: 248); and Baudelaire is, per Walter Benjamin, the painter of modern life. One major role of criticism today: to return all literature to that combination of Realism and Romance that gives us realism. In this respect criticism follows the example set for it by art (see note 2).

2 This is the perspective from which we can understand Jameson's remark that all modernisms end up, a generation later, as realisms—not as a cynical critique of the effectiveness of modernism's aspiration to Modernism, but as an observation of the tonic force of modernity's realism (its Realism, in short): the endless, perfecting tendency of the literary and cultural sphere to rediscover the geometrizing impulses of the modern worldview, which over time absorb any apparent ontological break in the universal—including the breaks of someone like Beckett, but also of, say, quantum physics—by treating it as a feature of a more complex system. The true radicalism and force of the modern worldview, which lies precisely in this capacity for adaptation, growth, and integration, might be understood as always a relation to and critique of a more Newtonian, common-sense version of that same modern world-view, to which it would relate as Reason (*Vernunft*) does, in Hegel, to Understanding (*Verstand*).

for instance). Clarifying Realism this way suggests that it is crucial to see the modes as philosophical and socially oriented preoccupations capable of organizing any kind of aesthetic production, and not as reifications of any single genre, medium, or form (the Romantic = the musical, the Modernist = the painterly, e.g.). From this perspective the history of any given social whole would need to be described as a series of negotiations between and arrangements of modes, with their own patterns of dominance, in which "the individual utterance cannot be considered without reference to the existing complex of norms"—a complex of norms that is particular to the social whole in question, and not necessarily to the modern period.[3]

What goes for the modes goes for the variables as well. The degree to which these variables appear to me as interesting and useful tools for literary comparison and literary history almost certainly owes a great deal to my focus on the modern period. They are thus to some extent products of the high visibility of the premodern-to-modern transition. That five of the six variables are primarily spatial, not temporal, may well be, for instance, an artifact of the modern-premodern shift—which would tell us something about the nature of that shift, if it were.

Shifting the focus to various moments in the spaces and time outside our recent adventure in modernity would presumably reveal the presence not only of different configurations of these six variables, but maybe the presence of completely *other* world-variables, ones that may be more difficult to see in this historical context because they do not change significantly over the premodern-modern break. Such variables might become visible through a

---

3 Jurij Tynjanov and Roman Jakobson, "Problems in the Study of Literature and Language," in *Readings in Russian Poetics*, ed. Ladislav Matejka and Krystyna Pomorska (Dalkey Archive, 2002), 80. The discussion here bears the imprint of conversation with Priya Joshi.

focus on other breaks, historical periods (inside or outside modernity), or forms of difference, which would highlight other transformations and changes: differences between literatures of city-states
and of monarchies; between those of polytheistic and of monothe-
istic societies (or indeed patterns specific to any mode of religious
and cosmographical practice); across one or another dynastic or
imperial transition; among polities oriented differently towards
subjection or domination; or between those of cultures whose basic
structures of trade and information are oriented on an East-West
axis, as opposed to a North-South one.[4] (None of these requires
abandoning the impulse to read literature historically, politically, or
sociologically, though some of it asks us to think about what those
concepts mean, and can mean.)

This leads to a proposal for one final variable, a variable of variables. Such a variable would describe, for any given moment, social
world, genre, or field of aesthetic production, the set of variables
that are subject to high levels of transformation, action, discussion, or negotiation, as well as those that pass largely unconsciously
through the labor of the artwork. By focusing our attention on the
variability of the variables as a system, such a variable of variables
would presumably allow for yet another level of socio-formal inter-

4 Consider in this context two possible examples: first, Nirvana Tanoukhi's discussion of the chronotopic force of African roads ("African Roads," *The Routledge Companion
to World Literature*, ed. Theo D'haen, David Damrosch, and Djelal Kadir [Routledge, 2012],
454–63). Second, in more detail, Eugene Y. Wang's description of the worldly imagination of an eighth-century Lotus Sutra tableau, located in the Mogao caves near Dunhuang,
China: "Behind the preaching Buddha is a cosmological view: surrounded by the sea
and encircled by the Iron Ring Mountains, the mushroom-shaped Mount Sumeru soars
upward, flaring out at the top. The cloud-rimmed Summit of Being conspicuously extends
beyond the delineated border of the illusionistic niche. The configuration thus openly
defies the spatial logic of illusionism the design has ostensibly built up. The recess is turned
inside out; depth rebounds to reassert the surface; and interiority becomes exteriority"
(*Shaping the Lotus Sutra: Buddhist Visual Culture in Medieval China* [U of Washington P,
2005], 310). Wang's discussion of the chronotope appears on 355.

pretation, whose overlap with the labor of the variables and the interactions of the modes would have to be made clear.

The variable of variables and the transhistorical application of the modal structure would allow for comparisons between various systems of the modes and the variables that expressed them, permitting both the analysis of patterns of movement and development at a meta-systemic level, and the study of far "smaller" units of likeness or difference. (Such analyses would, like this one, labor under all the conceptual difficulties posed to structuralism; they would benefit, likewise, from its conceptual advantages.)

This suggests in turn that the historical or transhistorical qualities of both the variables and the modes simply depend on the scale or level at which one locates one's analysis. Within the framework of the modern, Realism, Romanticism, and Modernism as I have used them here are essentially transhistorical concepts, which can then be specifically historicized (in relation to a transhistorical norm) in any smaller unit of analysis, whether that unit be a genre, a historical period, a formal strategy, a style, an oeuvre, or a work. At the same time, from a broader historical perspective, the modern versions of Realism, Romanticism, and Modernism *can themselves be historicized*, so long as one defines a transhistorical version of the modal concepts over and against their modern appearances (this transhistorical version could be, minimally, the one encoded by their logical relations: yes to the dominant world-view, phenomenological no to the dominant world-view, ontological no to the dominant world-view). Thus the danger that any concept here might be falsely codified as eternally transhistorical can be met by an awareness that the transhistorical, at least at the conceptual level, is essentially a matter of analytic scale, and can always be corrected or compensated for by a shift up or down the scalar ladder. Thus the seeming transhistorical unity of the Realist mode in the modern period can be disrupted and split by a focused attention on the varieties of Realism in various sub-modern locations *or* by an awareness of modern Realism's provincial relation to a supra-modern history in which modernity's version of, and relation to, Realism is just one of many players. The recognition that the relation between the historical and the transhistorical is essentially scalar (and a relation to the largest operative historical concept in the work) leads, then, not to a complacency about the inevitable limitations (and falsehoods) of the transhistorical, but to a heightened awareness of the choice of operative historical concepts as a fundamental decision in the practice of criticism. Not only here, but, finally, everywhere.

INDEX